Self-Study for Teacher Educators

"In *Self-Study for Teacher Educators*, Anastasia Samaras provides a compelling account of a teacher educator who serves as a model reflective practitioner for her teacher education students. Using her life experiences, her own teaching journals, and her students' journals and assignments, Samaras presents an account of her efforts to implement a sociocultural approach to teacher education based on the work of Vygotsky. The book documents her own evolution as a teacher educator and her students' reactions to her teaching. This autobiographical self-study provides a good example of the power of self-study research in improving teacher education practice. I highly recommend it to teacher educators."

—*Ken Zeichner, Hoefs-Bascom Professor of Teacher Education,*
University of Wisconsin-Madison

"This exciting and innovative book will assist teacher educators to reflect on their own practice. Samaras has interrogated pedagogy and practice within the social cultural perspective in such a way as to cause us to rethink the content and processes inherent to preservice teacher educators and continuing professional development with teachers in the field. For too long those involved in teacher education have not been exemplary role models for the pedagogy that they advocate. *Self-Study for Teacher Educators* demonstrates one professor's journey to effective teaching and learning, which we can all aspire to and learn from. It is essential reading for all those who want to reconceptualise their practice and make a valuable contribution to lifelong and lifewide learning."

—*Nicola Yelland, Professor, RMIT University , Melbourne, Australia*

"At the end of her study, Anastasia Samaras writes, 'Predetermined destinations do not lead us to new roads.' *Self-Study for Teacher Educators* presents a remarkable journey of self-discovery, a journey that leads from lessons learned while working in her father's Greek restaurant and from motherhood to Vygotskian principles for teacher education. Anastasia Samaras' message is that life is full of wonder and surprise and that joy can be found in teaching and in studying one's own practice."

—*Robert V. Bullough, Jr., Center for the Improvement of Teacher Education*
and Schooling (CITES), Brigham Young University

"In remarkable and compelling ways, Dr. Samaras uses Vygotskian principles to link the two domains about which I am most passionate: preservice teacher education and self-study of teacher education practices. The rich illustrations and novel perspectives will inspire important developments in teacher education."

—*Tom Russell, Queen's University, Canada*

Self-Study for Teacher Educators

Studies in the
Postmodern Theory of Education

Joe L. Kincheloe and Shirley R. Steinberg
General Editors

Vol. 190

PETER LANG
New York • Washington, D.C./Baltimore • Bern
Frankfurt am Main • Berlin • Brussels • Vienna • Oxford

Anastasia P. Samaras

Self-Study for Teacher Educators

Crafting a Pedagogy for Educational Change

PETER LANG

New York • Washington, D.C./Baltimore • Bern
Frankfurt am Main • Berlin • Brussels • Vienna • Oxford

Library of Congress Cataloging-in-Publication Data

Samaras, Anastasia P.
Self-study for teacher educators: crafting a pedagogy
for educational change / Anastasia P. Samaras.
p. cm. — (Counterpoints; vol. 190)
Includes bibliographical references.
1. Teachers—Training of. 2. Vygotskiæ, L. S. (Lev Semenovich),
1896–1934—Contributions in education. I. Title.
II. Counterpoints (New York, N.Y.); vol. 190.
LB1707 .S26   370'.71'1—dc21   00-067839
ISBN 0-8204-5299-8
ISSN 1058-1634

Die Deutsche Bibliothek-CIP-Einheitsaufnahme

Samaras, Anastasia P.:
Self-study for teacher educators: crafting a pedagogy
for educational change / Anastasia P. Samaras.
–New York; Washington, D.C./Baltimore; Bern;
Frankfurt am Main; Berlin; Brussels; Vienna; Oxford: Lang.
(Counterpoints; Vol. 190)
ISBN 0-8204-5299-8

Cover design by Dutton & Sherman Design
Author photo by Bill Denison

The paper in this book meets the guidelines for permanence and durability
of the Committee on Production Guidelines for Book Longevity
of the Council of Library Resources.

∞

© 2002 Peter Lang Publishing, Inc., New York

Printed in the United States of America

❖ *To Teddy*

❖ Credits

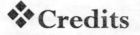

I am grateful to copyright holders for permission to reprint portions of my earlier writings.

Excerpts from "Scaffolds in the Field: Vygotskian Interpretation in a Teacher Education Program," by A. P. Samaras and S. Gismondi published in *Teaching and Teacher Education* 1998, are reprinted with permission from Elsevier Science, Ltd.

Figure 6.1 adapted from T. Hansen, L. Dirckinck-Holmfeld, R. Lewis, and J. Rigelj "Using Telematics for Collaborative Knowledge Construction," published in P. Dillenbourg, ed. 1999 *Collaborative Learning* page 186 is reprinted with permission from Elsevier Science, Ltd.

Excerpts from "When Is a Practicum Productive?: A Study in Learning to Plan," by A. P. Samaras published in *Action in Teacher Education* 2000, are reprinted with permission from the *Association of Teacher Educators*.

❖Table of Contents

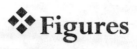

❖ Figures

Preface

Organization and Overview of the Book

The book is presented in three sections. In Part I, I present the case that it is critical for professors to practice self-study of their teaching practices in an effort to improve their students' learning. Like my students, I found that just talking about theory was not enough; in my case, it was essential for me to practice and model the theory of self-study for educators. Professors serve as role models for their students as they pose questions about their practice and seek answers to those questions through research and reflection. I share questions I posed about developing and using Vygotskian principles in my teaching. In preparation for writing this section, I examined my graduate studies and the university context that enabled me to try out my theory in practice. As I wrote, however, I realized that my Vygotskian orientations were rooted much earlier.

As I moved from my training in quantitative research to a narrative inquiry style and began to write not only for others but also for myself, I gained new insights about my teaching. Finding like-minded communities in which to share and refine my work helped me sort through the theories that inform my teaching. But did the theories I subscribed to translate into practice in my classrooms? In other words, did my teaching have integrity? I found that the theoretical model for my teaching grew out of my cultural context: my intellectual experiences, my relationships and interactions, and the historical-political era of teacher education that encircled me. Self-knowledge enabled me to better understand how my model for teaching grew.

Throughout the book, I tell of life lessons relevant to my teaching using an autobiographical self-study approach. I use the word *self-study* to mean critical examination of one's actions and the context of those actions in order to achieve a more conscious mode of professional activity, in contrast to action based on habit, tradition, and impulse. This model of learning involves mind, body, and spirit. I see my past education and work experiences as an integrally connected set of influences on my teaching today.

Self-study is more than an exploration of one's self. The heart of self-study is the application of the knowledge one gains through this process to one's teaching practices. Berlak and Berlak (1987) state that "only as we come to view our own actions and preferences, as products of historical as well as biographical forces, rather than as natural and inevitable, can we escape the ideological assumptions that underlie teaching practices, and engage in reflective teaching" (175). My autobiographical self-study inquiry led to a deep questioning about why I profess and practice this model.

I share snapshots of who I am through portraits of myself as a student, teacher, researcher, and teacher educator. In addition to sharing my experiences as a teacher, I use my experiences as a learner at school and a worker in my family's restaurant to illustrate how Vygotskian notions worked organically to shape my teaching philosophy and practice today. As I revisit my steps in a retrospective inquiry, I use an introspective writing style to enable you to be included in my backward mapping.

In Part II, I explain my work context and my efforts to reshape the pre–student teaching experience by structuring ways for preservice teachers to learn by doing in real classrooms, gather support from peers and teachers, and learn how to mentor each other as they develop their own understandings of how to practice the craft of teaching. I offer a description of four Vygotskian principles that I have found most relevant in guiding preservice teachers' development in becoming teachers. I share how I have applied those principles in my own classroom as I crafted a pedagogy for educational change. I discuss the need to change the shape of teacher education classrooms and programs by merging educational theories with educational practice.

In Part III, I describe two case studies using a Vygotskian model, one inside and one outside the given realm of a teacher education classroom. The first is a case study of two pairs of preservice teachers, one pair who worked with an exemplary cooperating teacher and the other pair who worked with a cooperating teacher who was less than exemplary. I summarize research about my teaching in which I analyze the ways in which the Vygotskian model has influenced preservice teachers' perceptions about teaching. In the second case study, I invite you to think about the application of Vygotskian theory beyond the teacher education classroom. I share the insights I have gained from forming interdisciplinary partnerships with faculty in a school of arts and sciences in the areas of dance, biology, and drama. Those creative experiences allowed me to learn and think in new ways and to model working with multiple zones of proximal development.

Last, I explore the implications of using self-study and Vygotskian principles in teaching and the benefits of such work to both students and professors.

Need for This Book

This writing is particularly timely in an era of educational reform that calls for new approaches to designing programs of teacher education. It addresses the need for supportive structures and a culture that invites preservice teachers into the community of the teaching profession. In the context of the need to provide enough teachers of good quality, the turnover from teacher retirement, and the high attrition rates of beginning teachers, especially in high-poverty schools, educators must rethink the ways they prepare, assess, and induct teachers. Now more than ever, educators are recognizing that preservice teachers need opportunities to test their theories and construct personal knowledge about teaching in dynamic and mentoring environments. They need spaces to reflect on and study their practices. A strong theoretical and conceptual foundation helps explain why strategies work or don't work. But preservice teachers also need professors who model the practice of reflection and self-study in their own teaching practices.

Vygotsky considered schools to be the best "cultural laboratories" to study thinking or social settings specifically designed to modify thinking. Schools and programs of education can also be cultural laboratories; I explain how my education-related life experiences have shaped the development of my practical theory. This connection helps explain my attraction to Vygotskian principles of learning. The fact that I am continuously engaged in the construction and reconstruction of my own knowledge as I attempt to improve teacher education is more important to me than which theories I integrate in my own work. When teacher educators articulate their practical theories, no matter what their personal theory base, they model for their students a necessary professional inquiry—curriculum belongs to teachers, after all. We choose our theories of how to teach. This creative ownership of the curriculum will be an invaluable asset in coping with the current approach to education reform, which relies all too heavily on high-stakes testing.

Related Literature

Although there are a few books available about using a Vygotskian approach to teach children in elementary classrooms, nothing has been written about using a Vygotskian approach in teacher education classrooms. The early literature focused on childhood education. For example, in 1995, Berk and Winsler wrote an excellent book, *Scaffolding Children's Learning: Vygotsky and Early Childhood Education*. In 1996, Bodrova and Leong wrote *Tools of the Mind: The Vygotskian Approach to Early Childhood Education*. Dixon-Krauss's *Vygotsky in the Classroom: Mediated Literacy Instruction and Assessment* (1996) is a textbook for teaching children, with a focus on literacy instruction. Moll (1990) notes in his edited book, *Vygotsky and Education*, that he found no work that applied Vygotsky's theory to instruction. His book does not include the topic of the preparation of preservice teachers. Tharp and Gallimore (1988) wrote *Rousing Minds to Life* and began a very important discussion for inservice teacher training. Their research deals with individual consulting, training, and action research projects for teachers' staff development, with an emphasis on verbal mediation to express teachers' implicit theories of teaching and learning.

In terms of research articles, although there is related research, there is no comprehensive model for the organization of teacher education coursework and fieldwork. For example, Manning and Payne (1993) wrote articles about using a Vygotskian-based theory for teacher education but with a focus on one Vygotskian concept; that is, higher mental functioning in relation to preservice teachers' metacognition and self-regulation for planning. Gallimore, Dalton, and Tharp (1986) and Au (1990) conducted neo-Vygotskian research on cognitive activity and metacognition, and Edwards (1995) examined the essential role of the cooperating teacher in that process. Other researchers have noted that new forms of teacher education assessment are needed (Dalton 1989; Wineburg 1997).

Cognitive psychologists have written about Vygotskian notions such as "socially shared cognition" in teaching elementary school children (Resnick, Levine, and Teasley 1991) and in designing learning communities (Brown 1994). While there have been calls for a Vygotskian approach in teacher education (Hausfather 1996), no books to date have been written on such an approach to help teachers in their preparation.

Uses of the Book

The primary audiences for this book are professionals interested in the improvement of the education of teachers. This includes, but is not limited to:

- self-study teacher educators
- action researchers
- teacher educators
- educational anthropologists
- coordinators of education programs
- directors of teacher education
- supervisors of preservice teachers' field experiences
- university and school administrators, deans of education, such as chairs, principals, and superintendents
- content specialists who share the responsibility for teaching preservice teachers
- graduate students of education, administration, educational and cognitive psychology, cultural studies, and human development
- researchers and students investigating sociocultural theory in general and/or its specific applications to teacher education
- researchers interested in education-related life histories and autobiographical inquiry

Other relevant audiences include:

- curriculum specialists
- accreditation directors and other evaluators of teacher education programs
- directors and officers of learned societies and professional organizations who help formulate policy about how teachers are prepared and assessed and how that preparation may influence how children are taught and assessed
- policymakers and lawmakers at all levels of government
- general audiences interested in an inside look at the work of teachers and teacher educators

❖ Acknowledgments

I did not write this book alone. As you read through it, you will learn of the interpersonal relationships in my life course that made this book possible. Indeed, I agree with van der Veer and Valsiner (1991) that it was intellectual interdependence that brought my creative expressions into being and action. As you learn of my cultural history, the world that has surrounded me, and the bounty of mentors who have embraced and inspired me, you will see that I could not begin to thank all the people who helped me to construct this book.

I gratefully acknowledge all the students and teachers who made this work possible. Pseudonyms were used for names of students, cooperating teachers, and schools. I wish to acknowledge the work of my students Ann Walker Korahais and Ellen Dwan O'Leary and thank them for permission to include their concept maps in the text. Special thanks and credit to photographer Bill Denison for reminding me that I don't always have to be so serious.

This work would not have been possible without the support received from The Catholic University of America, Washington, D.C. That support included professional travel grants, faculty research grants, a sabbatical leave, and technical assistance from Michelle Papadopoulos and Andrew Boyd at the Center for Planning and Information Technology. I especially thank the many people associated with Peter Lang Publishing, whose collaborative efforts, directed by Christopher S. Myers, made it possible for me to share this story with you. I extend special appreciation to Sophie Appel for her coordination of its publication. I am forever grateful to Bob Bullough for his thoughtful guidance and redirection of an earlier writing. Kate Babbitt's developmental editorship and mentorship enabled me to weave my personal story with pedagogy and helped me bring this book to fruition.

I hope that the lamplighters of my splendid journey will recognize themselves in these pages. I give many thanks to all of them. My social and cognitive world has been enriched through magnificent collaborative adventures and the love I have shared with my many students, advisors, colleagues, Greta's Girls, friends, and family. My children and husband have inspired me to persevere on this most challenging writing and are a wondrous blessing. My greatest insights have come from them. I thank each of you from the bottom of my heart.

Reference

van der Veer, R., and J. Valsiner. 1991. *Understanding Vygotsky: A quest for synthesis.* Cambridge, Mass: Blackwell.

❖ Lev Semyonovich Vygotsky

(1896–1934)

Lev Vygotsky (1896–1934), a renowned Russian developmental psychologist, believed that humans are significantly influenced by the sociocultural, or social and historical, context that mediates their experience (Wertsch 1985). Accordingly, in order to teach children, we must understand the social, cultural, and societal contexts in which they develop (Berk and Winsler 1995). Although Vygotsky was influenced by Marxist theory, he diverged from Marxian thinking when he stated that the first problem is to show how an "individual response emerges from the forms of collective life" (Vygotsky [1960] 1981, 165); that is, man is more than a product of history and circumstance because he can use psychological tools to transform nature and himself. Contrary to Glassman (2001), Vygotsky considered the source of change to be the individual, although within a social community. Vygotsky emphasized that it is in the context of social and goal-directed activities in which individual development is advanced (Vygotsky [1934] 1962, 1978) and where man changes himself and his culture. Bruner (1987) describes him as a cultural theorist who saw education as a way to improve individual potential as well as the "historical expression and growth of the human culture from which Man springs" (2). Vygotsky investigated various levels of human development including phylogenesis, ontogenesis, and microgenesis.

Second, Vygotsky believed that participation in authentic cultural activities is necessary for development to occur. Human mental functioning can be socially shared or socially situated through interaction found in dyads, cohorts, or other small groups (Wertsch 1991). Vygotsky recognized children's individual consciousness and not just consciousness as influenced by children's changing social relationships (El'Konin 1968). He believed that the personal activity of the student was the base of the education process. The learner's participation in authentic cultural activities is critical for development.

Third, Vygotsky held that mental processes can be understood only if we understand the tools, especially language, that mediate them. Tools, and human use of tools, are products of sociocultural evolution and are inherently situated in social interactional, cultural, institutional, and historical context (Wertsch, 1985). Higher mental functions involve the use of language and other cultural mediators to advance self-regulated thought processes.

Fourth, Vygotsky believed that formal education could impact development. He believed that although the developmental level of the student should be a factor of consideration, education could promote development if teachers challenged and assisted students' problem-solving through formative assessment procedures. His theory of the origins of higher mental functions in joint or collective engagement with dialogue and mediation has relevance to culturally mediated practices for teacher education.

The four Vygotskian principles I have found essential in preparing preservice teachers are: (1) Social and cultural influences shape development; (2) Learning occurs during situated and joint activity; (3) Cognition is always socially mediated, especially through language; and (4) Education leads development. Each of these principles will be discussed in subsequent chapters as they relate to my work in teaching teachers. I foresee a greater use of these and other Vygotskian ideas in teacher education.

Vygotsky, too, was influenced by the social and historical context of his life and historical era. He was born into a middle-class religious Jewish family in Orsha, Belorussia, and grew up in Gomel. His father, Semyon L'vock Vygodsky, was a bank manager, and his mother, Cecilia Moiseievna, had been a teacher. Vygotsky was the second child; he had one older sister, four younger sisters, and two younger brothers. One brother died of tuberculosis at 14 years old and the other died of typhus. His mother also had tuberculosis, which Vygotsky contracted and fought for many years (Valsiner and van der Veer, 2000).

His interest in the emotions of art and theater; his mother's love of poetry; the intellectual, cultural, and caring atmosphere of his home; and his private tutor's pursuit in developing independent thinkers in his students each shaped Vygotsky's zone of proximal development. He lived in a time marked by political turbulence and social idealism; politicians and researchers alike believed they could remake Russian society in the early decades of the twentieth century. Although Jews were discriminated against in higher education, Vygotsky's giftedness and good fortune earned him a place at Moscow University and Shaniavsky People's University. In 1917, he graduated from Moscow University with a law degree while also studying psychology, linguistics, social science, art, literature, and philosophy at Shaniavsky People's University. He brought each of these studies to bear in his thinking about development. Afterward, he was a teacher in Gomel (where he had grown up), where he taught high school literature and lectured on psychology, art history, the psychology of art, and theater in various schools. His position teaching psychology at Gomel's teacher training school gave him opportunities to work with developmentally disabled children, who he believed were not taught to their potentials.

In 1924, he gave a dynamic speech on reflexological and psychological investigations at the Second All-Russian Psychoneurological Congress in Leningrad that earned him a prominent position at the Institute for Psychology in Moscow, although he was never formally trained in psychology (Wertsch 1985). He also worked at the Institute of Defectology or Mental Retardation and Special Education. His study circles, particularly the two other members of the troika of revolutionary scientists in the Vygotskian school of thought—Aleksandr Romanovich Luria (1902–1977) and Aleksei Nikolaevich Leont'ev (1904–1979)—led to his conception of the sociocultural theory that he hoped would refashion Russian society (Newman and Holzman 1993).

Much of Vygotsky's work was not known in the West until the 1960s and after Stalin's death. One of his most famous works about sociocultural theory, *Thought and Language* (1934), was suppressed by Stalin's administration from 1936–1956 and was published in English only in 1962. In 1960, *The Genesis of Higher Mental Functions* was first published in Moscow. In 1978, *Mind and Society,* a collection of Vygotsky's papers, was published in English.

The work of Vygotsky was suppressed by guardians of Marxist thinking, who misunderstood his work on metacognition and the role of consciousness in development to mean autonomous consciousness (Bruner 1985,1987). The Stalinist party banned Vygotsky's work partly because they viewed his connection with bourgeois scholars as a threat to the regime and partly because they distrusted him as a Jew (Bruner 1987). Vygotsky often cited works of German, French, Swiss, and American researchers in his lectures. Translations and dissemination of his work in the West were slowed by the economic and political conditions of the Soviet Union, the Cold War era, and the popularity of Piagetian and behaviorist theories of education (Berk and Winsler 1996).

In his short life of only 38 years, which ended with tuberculosis, he wrote prolifically and left a plethora of papers that would be read across the world many years later (see van der Veer and Valsiner 1991 for Vygotsky's complete writings). His diverse research left a legacy of ideas that would be extended and interpreted by researchers and theorists from many disciplines (Kozulin 1999) and across cultures (Jacob 1992). This book is one such extension and interpretation of his work for teacher education.

Part I. Introduction

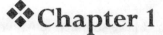# ❖ Chapter 1

Beyond Traditional Practices

Logbook, 2 January 1999

The New Year had finally come. Following the tradition that had been passed down to me by my mother, I grabbed the broom and ran to the front door to sweep out the old and bring in the new. Then I took a pot and wooden spoon and banged the pot loudly at my front door to celebrate the newness and opportunity for renewal in a new year. "Happy New Year!" I shouted again and again. As I did, I heard my 80-year-old mother, who lives down the street, banging her pot and shouting and laughing out loud like a madwoman to whomever could hear her, "Happy New Year! Happy New Year!" I laughed at our mutual silliness yet rejoiced for the opportunity to hear her cheery voice and happiness for another year. I placed this vision safely in my memory for the day I knew that would inevitably come when I would hear her voice only in my thoughts.

What a beautiful life and how beautiful tradition can make it. Yet I both loved and hated traditions in my life. I saw "traditional" as being or doing what was the given thing to do, and I eschewed being typical. Getting married when one graduated from college was so typical for women in my time. I married during college. My mother worried that I would never graduate. My father wondered why I didn't have children right away.

Nevertheless, I became a teacher, which was such a traditional and typical profession for women. I constantly tried to move away from the norm in my teaching. Whenever I had the courage to step outside the given realm of teaching, I could feel that I mattered to my students, which constantly renewed my life work as an educator. Like shifting to a high note in a predictable melody, I felt vibrant when I altered my typical stance to see the possible. When I became a teacher educator, I observed how teachers were being taught—the methods were so traditional and ineffective. Would I change or reshape any of that tradition as a teacher educator?

Where shall I begin? I have so much to tell you. Let me begin where I began as I wrote this book. As a teacher educator and practicing theoretician, I have designed and utilized a Vygotskian, or socioculturally based, model for preparing preservice teachers. I have been assessing the effectiveness of this innovation. I have been working to change the shape of teacher education by studying the effects of my practice when I use this model (Samaras 1998a). As Vygotsky did in his historical context, I am attempting to develop concrete solutions to realities in education that are grounded in more than theoretical rhetoric. Vygotsky viewed psychology as more than a scientific study of education. According to Leont'ev and Luria (1968), Vygotsky demanded that psychology "go beyond abstract theoretical knowledge and intervene in human life to actively help in shaping it…A psychologist cannot but be a thinker, but he has to be a practitioner too" (367).

Since there are multiple components of teacher preparation, and multiple ways to refine it, I present my work as only one model of how to improve the way teachers can be prepared. The approach can be modified and expanded to fit your particular context. I see myself as an artistic researcher creating a portrait, not a prescription, for teacher education.

It is not unusual for me to place my now-explicit theories of teaching within the context of my past. My pen and computer have served as my shovels to dig down to the roots of what I have personally come to believe about teaching preservice teachers. I especially write to hear my voice out there on the other end, not unlike playing a note and then hearing its sound. That is, I tell because it moves me to see who I am becoming as a teacher educator. In line with Vygotskian concepts, I understand myself only when I have tried out my words on the social other (Valsiner and van der Veer 2000). I tell of the lessons I learned along the way that impacted my heart and mind as a teacher and moved me toward the development of a Vygotskian model for teacher education.

When I began to write about using and studying the model, I recognized that something was missing. I asked myself, "Why Vygotsky? Why was I attracted to this theory?" One of Vygotsky's basic themes is that higher mental functioning and individual cognition are derived from social life. He insisted that an individual's historical, cultural, and institutional context was an important factor in his or her intellectual development. In order to understand the individual, one must first understand the social context in which the individual exits (Wertsch 1985). What were the cultural forces that shaped me and affected my beliefs about teaching? Kincheloe (1991) calls this the dialectic of distance; it allows one to view oneself in relationship to wider social and ideological forces. In a Vygotskian sense, I too am a knower who exists in a sociohistorical context that influenced the way that I understand the phenomena I investigate. According to Wertsch and Younnis (1987), the fact that the investigator is a person within a sociohistorical and cultural tradition is central to how phenomena are defined.

Through using autobiographical self-study, I was able to reconstruct the critical incidents in my education-related life history that led me to profess and practice a Vygotskian approach in preparing teachers. As I sorted out the sources of my teaching theory and practice, I moved toward an interpretation of the lived relationship between my education-related life experiences and my efforts to learn to teach preservice teachers from a sociocultural perspective. The conceptualization of my model matured in my work at The Catholic University of America (CUA), although the chrysalis of my model was formed in my youth. For three decades, I have taught, consulted, and conducted research in junior and senior high schools, preschools, at a university laboratory school, in Head Start programs, at a community college, and at numerous universities. This book offers both my interpretation of how to use and assess a Vygotskian model in preparing preservice teachers and a self-study of how that model became central to my teaching.

I have found self-study to be a difficult yet emancipating process. Somehow, I was always drawn toward self-study of my teaching practices, although it was not part of my teacher training. It just seemed to be what I did. I found that telling my own story helped me understand my teaching better (Samaras 1995), but I wanted to be sure that I told more than merely my story; I didn't want a narcissist psychoanalytic self-analysis. I reveal myself in this book to model how preservice teachers and professors can tell their own stories to help them understand how their early life lessons shaped their teaching and their perspectives about students who are not like them. I believe you have to be willing to tell the truth about your own life if you want students to tell their truths. I look at what I am doing and the effects, or the "so what," of my work for students, as I hope they will one day do with their own students.

As a novice academician, I struggled to articulate my understanding of integrating, not merely connecting, theory and practice. The process was hindered because I was not speaking through my personal narrative. As Brodkey (1996) expressed, "the power of the rules" can rob learners of the pleasures of their intellectual work. I was encouraged by colleagues not to use a self-study research approach; I was seeking tenure at the time, and self-study had not yet earned legitimacy as an academic approach. Nonetheless, I continued to use a self-study approach in my research, and over time I found my own kind in circles of self-study. As I read the work of other self-study professors, I knew I was no longer alone, although I continued to personally sort out what self-study meant to my teaching (Samaras 1995, 1997, 1998b).

In 1999, Zeichner wrote that "the birth of the self-study in teacher education movement around 1990 has been probably the single most significant development ever in the field of teacher education research" (8). The Self-Study of Teacher Education Practices Special Interest Group (S-STEP SIG) of the American Education Educational Research Association, established in 1992, struggles with "a" definition of self-study, partially because of its diverse methodologies and applications in varied educational settings. For example, until recently there were no guidelines for autobiographical self-study (Bullough and Pinnegar 2001).

Teacher educators can attest to the common wisdom that professional development is an ongoing and evolving process for all teachers. Fewer teacher educators, however, have acknowledged that self-study is a legitimate form of research toward that professional development, not only for school-based teachers but also for themselves. I am a firm believer in practicing what I profess, in modeling what I teach. I maintain that the process of inquiry must begin with the professor's self-study.

I practice a reflective writing process that is similar to the one I ask my students to engage in. That is, I retrace how I arrived at my personal assumptions about teaching and learning through a backward mapping. In my determination to go forward, I needed to look back so I could recall where I have been. Like Theseus in the ancient story of the Minotaur, I too feel like I have been in a labyrinth, taking the seemingly wrong paths, often without any clues or without anyone to lead me through the maze. But like Theseus, who was advised by Ariadne, a wise and tenderhearted young maiden, to use a spool of golden thread to guide him back through the labyrinth, I have used the thread of retrospection to guide me home.

At times I have been lonely and confused and have searched desperately for companions. I see now that I found many treasures, sometimes when I was alone but most often with others, as I explored teaching from a sociocultural perspective. My beliefs about learning and teaching that first surfaced were very clear. Events of high personal importance typically produce vivid and accurate memories in retrospective recall (Bower 1992; Conway and Beckerian 1988). The purpose of the journey back in time was to identify some of the major links and themes in my teaching experiences and life experiences. Woven throughout my journey backward are some of my important life lessons; these told me much about why I was drawn to Vygotsky.

Being of an analytical nature, I often recorded professional logs and revisited my inquiries about teaching in an effort to improve it. I include excerpts from those logs throughout this book. As Taylor (1998) suggests in reflective-practitioner research, I integrate my logbooks in this book to document the work as I experienced it. Some of the logs are my private speech or conversations with myself about the concerns and questions I had as they arose. My perceptions and observations, as well as those of my students, drove the research and the analyses of the process, inviting action. I also include excepts from my self-study, portions of my autobiography that illustrate the points I am making in the book. Finally, I include excerpts from the research my students conducted about their teaching and their perceptions of the ways I use Vygotskian principles. The result of my investigation of personal and practical knowledge was that I came to know and understand classroom life through my autobiographical accounts and research. These accounts, as Britzman (1991) has suggested, are useful because they give authority to the meanings I derive from my story and a sense of ownership for the knowledge I constructed as I made theory from my life (see Belenky, Clinchy, Goldberger, and Tarule 1986). My critical thinking about the broad historical forces of culture, class, and gender that both constricted and positively shaped my teaching has enabled me to feel in charge of my own professional life. This is not unlike what Kincheloe (1991) talks about in the emancipation that comes between the knower and the known or the researcher to their research. There is no knowledge without the knower. The perspective of the researcher must be granted the same seriousness and attention as the research design.

Although I have used Vygotsky to center my work, I am becoming my own theoretician. As Langer (1953) notes, artistic experiences are always in a state of becoming. Zeichner and Liston (1996) discuss the importance of teachers' practical and personal theorizing, which I extend to teacher educators:

> Traditional teacher educators take the view that teachers practice but do not theorize. The important point here is that accepting the idea of teachers as reflective practitioners involves recognition of the role of teachers in the production of theoretical knowledge about teaching through their practice. The process of reflection, in which teachers make more conscious and articulate those practical theories implicit in their practice and subject them to critique, can be considered a form of educational theorizing. This practical and personal theorizing offers an insider's perspective on teaching and learning in schools that cannot be gained from theories invented by outsiders (38).

I have been mentored by my academic advisors and have experienced social mediation in my own life. I include those thoughts throughout this book. Now I move away from using only Vygotsky's words as I tell of my teaching. I am developing my voice as I suggest practices in keeping with my intentions and values (see Bakhtin 1981; Ball 2000). This process will help me move my students toward formulating their own theories rather than simply parroting mine. I can better understand now where my students must pass because I have journeyed there. I am a practicing theoretician, modeling and studying theory in practice. I have enjoyed this writing more than any other I have ever done. Come walk with me.

My Education Autobiography

As I look back, I can see the seeds of my values as an educator, a feminist, a caretaker, a humanist, and a bicultural Greek American in my childhood and young adulthood. Each of these identities is so important in my work as an educator, and each of them is an integral part of me because of my life experiences. I did not try them on for size as an experiment; they passed through my body and became part of my being. The memories that follow are part of my own process of self-study.

There are six children in our Pantelides family: three boys and three girls. I am the third oldest child and the first girl. My parents were instrumental in the formation of my cultural and ethnic identity (see Portes 2001) as I also learned to function in the dominant culture. They made sure we shared their high valuation of education: All six of us graduated from college, and three of us became teachers with graduate degrees. Going to college was not a choice for us; it was the ticket to a better quality of life. My father, Savvas Hadjipanteli, came to America as a teenager during the 1920s from the village of Yialousa, Cyprus. My dad was named after his uncle, who was a teacher who traveled from village to village by donkey to teach. He left his beautiful island of Cyprus and came with his older brother to America in search of the "American dream." His dream was to provide a better life for his family and for his children to become educated professionals. I think he viewed this dream as an opportunity, but knew he had to make things happen. He was right. Not all immigrants found the United States to be a welcoming place. My husband's Greek immigrant family experienced racial and ethnic tensions in Maryland firsthand. The Ku Klux Klan forced the closure of their family restaurant in Cambridge in the 1920s. They defaced the building, poured sour milk on its walls, and stood posted with shotguns outside its doors until they left town.

But my dad's voyage to America brought him to the port of Baltimore, where he lived and worked with other young Greek men until he went into the U.S. Army. After his military service, he was introduced to my mother, Magdalene Comsudis, who lived in Iselin, New Jersey. After a short courtship, they were married and came to Annapolis to raise their family.

I heard many immigrant stories from my dad. He demanded that I listen to his stories; that was his way of teaching. He explained so many times how we were related to others in our Greek community. Knowing our family roots was very important to him. He told of his first job in the United States, where he worked for $3.50 a week as a counter boy at Nick's Restaurant on N. Linden Avenue in Baltimore. Two years later, he became manager of the restaurant while he moonlighted on Saturdays as a window-washer for 25¢ a day. His poverty bred skills of determination, resourcefulness, and creativity that I could recognize at a young age. He eventually bought his own restaurant, but he had to sell it to join the army in 1941, where he served until 1946. When he married my mother, he came to Annapolis, Maryland to be with his brother and raise his family in a small town on the water. With the generous assistance of Steve Foundas and Alex Patrides, he received housing and an installment plan to buy the Royal Restaurant, which he ran for many years. These stories told of the importance of seeking support from others and of collaboration.

People had been generous to him, and he was in turn generous to many others. My father told of how Greeks had sponsored his entry into the United States and how he had sponsored others. Each new immigrant arrival was helped by fellow Greeks to find housing and a job and to establish himself financially and then try to bring his family from the Old Country. I watched our Greek community grow over time, and in particular the Cyprian Greek constituency, which my father was very instrumental in establishing. He taught me about these bonds of family, friendship, and obligation. In 1970, the local newspaper ran his story in an article titled "Faith, Hard Work, Help of Friends—Formula for Success" (*Anne Arundel Times,* 23 April 1970). In another newspaper article, he said, "We all help one another in need. We form a very close relationship. We are together in sad times and in happiness. We feel like one big family—the Greeks in Annapolis. Not just Annapolis, really, the whole country" (*The Sunday Sun*, 11 December 1977).

I remember my father as a mover and a shaker, a critically outspoken leader in the church, which was conveniently located one block from our house. Our house was always filled with action; we always had loads of company and frequently broke bread with friends and strangers. I too would be involved in our church as a Sunday school teacher and as director of the first Greek folk dance troupe that performed for church festivals. I served as the entertainment chair and master of ceremonies for church fundraisers and community service events that required a great deal of organizing, coordinating, working with people, and speaking impromptu to large audiences. My father always used to say that whatever skills I learned at the restaurant and in life I would carry with me in my future work, but I couldn't imagine how.

My mother was born to a poor immigrant family who first settled in New York City in a dumbbell-type tenement house where the cheaper units faced each other and looked into the courtyard where she played. When my mother was 18 years old, she joined my Greek-Macedonian grandmother in the New York City furrier district; the fur industry employed many Greeks. She worked long hours in a sweatshop, where her mother apprenticed her in the craft of finishing fur coats. Along with many other Greek women, my Grandmother Anastasia was recruited to the sewing trade because she did not need to speak English to do her work, she knew how to sew, and she knew to do what she was supposed to do.

The unskilled Greek women learned of the work mainly by word of mouth from family and friends. Furrier contractors also ran job advertisements in local Greek newspapers sold in Greek neighborhoods in New York City. Greek and Jewish men stretched the animal skins, nailed the pelts to patterns, and then sewed the large fur pieces together. Then the women sewed the coat linings and did the finishing by hand. My grandmother and mother worked hard and didn't complain. When my grandmother died young of cancer, my mother did her best to take care of her family.

The labor movement was alive and well in the 1930s. My mother recalls the incident that happened before she began work in the sweatshop when the unions threw a stink bomb in the window of her mother's shop. In an oral history, I asked her if she wasn't scared when she then went to work there in 1938, and she replied, "I was 18 years old; I didn't know any better. It was a security and we were glad to have a job. We also didn't want to pay union dues, although I never found out how much the dues were." She and her coworkers were able to take piecework home to make extra money, which they desperately needed. The Greeks were a source of strength to the garment industry. And however difficult the conditions in the United States might be, they were still better than conditions in the Old World.

My mother tells of how she sang Greek folk songs with the other women to pass the time of tedious work in a shop filled with tiny fur particles they inhaled all day long. Her boss was a contractor who sent the goods to a manufacturer and hired nonunion workers to save money. He kept a close watch on any union stirrings, and when organizers approached the shop, he would bolt the doors and turn off the lights and they would pretend no one was there. They sat in silence and stiffened when they heard the organizers knock at the door. When the workers had to go to the restroom, they quickly ran down the hallway and the door was quickly rebolted. My Aunt Mary, who stayed in the furrier business, told me that she never knew what was waiting for her when she got done with work. She was often harassed and feared union retaliation. I remember visiting her shop as a teenager and hearing the chattering and smiling Greek voices in the community of furriers.

My mom is musical, artistic, animated, and overjoyed to learn new things—almost childlike. We would go on trips to New York City to visit my stylish and beautiful Aunt Mary, see shows at Radio City Hall, embrace the high fashion, and taste the drama the Big Apple affords. I often heard stories of my mother's relatives who were actors and sculptors. It was all very different from our pastoral quaint Annapolis residence and my father's relatives who came from the villages of Cyprus. I loved both of these worlds.

For the most part, life was good and rich in many ways for our family. We had an extended family, a church community, and many acquaintances through our family restaurant. We lived in an active neighborhood. There was a large apartment complex next to us where our best childhood friends lived. A pharmacy was located one block to the left of our house. There was a movie house two blocks away that we often frequented. Our elementary school was located downtown and was about a fifteen-minute walk from our house.

When my dear sisters and I look at old family photos of our West Street home and backyard, we compare what we see in the photographs with our memories and they don't seem to match. We see that our living arrangements were more shabby than we remembered, but we never saw that then. We didn't feel ashamed of who we were then, nor do we now. Compared with many other Greek families in town, we were relatively rich.

We enjoyed playing in the large parking lot in back of our house that emptied at 5:00 P.M. We played kickball there every single evening. Our house was always filled with noisy children and birthday parties. The front of our house had the best seat in town for the city parades. I remember jumping out of bed and running out of the house when I heard the brass bands and the African-American drum and bugle corps. I loved marching alongside the bands, stepping in rhythm for many blocks with the majorettes, and then running back home. As the musicians became more distant, I could hear the high notes of the vertical xylophones fade after a set of songs. I delighted in the drummers' repetitive rhythms between song sets. I looked forward to this cycle of Memorial Day and summer day parades. One day I would coach the school drill team and my sons would teach me to play African drums.

As a young child at home, I played restaurant and other themes using the wide newspaper sheets and fat pencils that Mr. Morris handed my sister Renee and me through his newspaper office window. I always tried to see him better, but I could only see his arm and hear his low voice through the long half-opened school-like window that was situated above our heads in our backyard. I remember writing and drawing with Renee a lot. The newspaper company eventually bought our house in order to expand their office. They ran an advertisement in their newspaper that read "This house has got to go!" Someone paid to move our house to a nearby lot. I still see my house when I take walks in the neighborhood. It is now located on the once-empty field where we played kickball until the private-school kids who lived in the better neighborhood in back of us said we couldn't play there anymore. They knew the owner.

In 1958, I was a third-grader at Annapolis Elementary School in the first integrated classroom in Anne Arundel County. I had the only African-American teacher in the school. This teacher cared for me. The most important lesson Mrs. Johnston taught me was that nurturance matters in learning. I had felt that my abilities were weaker than those of my classmates in grades one and two, and her belief in my abilities in grade three allowed me to shine and feel good about who I was.

Even many years later, whenever she saw my mother, she would ask how I was doing. I remember the last day of school in her class. We were lined up at the door to get our report cards, and she bent down and kissed me on the cheek, as she did with each child who would accept it. Her embrace seemed an unusual, but welcoming, behavior for a teacher. No one seemed to treat her differently in the school, even though she was black. I was aware that this teacher was like no other I had ever had before, but my parents didn't seem bothered by it because she was a good teacher. So I didn't feel uneasy about her either. Furthermore, she was so kind to me. My mother had had African-American teachers when she was a student in New York City and had gone to school with African-American children. My father employed many African Americans at the restaurant, and my associations with "the help" taught me not to be afraid of them as other white children might be. I felt privileged to have opportunities to deal with diversity that my friends did not have.

During this time, African Americans, Jews, Greeks, and Catholics were not allowed to join some beaches, clubs, and boatyards in Annapolis. Segregation was widespread in our small conservative town. In that respect, it was easy to relate to other ethnic communities who worked and lived near us and had similar occupational profiles. Many years later, I would be invited to talk about those experiences (Samaras 1984, 1994a). As I spoke to Anne Arundel County public school teachers, I struggled to explain my attraction to and pull away from my ethnicity so they might understand the tensions their immigrant students might experience.

My story illustrates the tug-of-war among those of my family's heritage, who longed to hold on to the values of their culture while they also tried to immerse themselves in the new American culture they were living in. My parents were intent on keeping us with other Greeks. When I was 7 years old, I was invited to attend an acting school in Chicago. My father's response was, "Is it a Greek acting school? Will you learn to speak Greek and learn of your Greek heritage there?"

I am a white American girl. I am also an olive-skinned Greek American girl. I didn't mind when my classmates shortened my long name to "Annie," but in college I took back my Greek name. I live in Annapolis, but I also live in a smaller circle of my Greek-American community, which dominates my social life through church events, dances, and intergenerational parties. I like both worlds, but my Greek-American world limits my time and interactions in my American world, and this became extremely problematic during my adolescent years. Sometimes I would have a brief interlude to attend American teenage parties, but work, Greek friends, and family always took priority. I didn't feel discriminated against like the African Americans in my town because we were not as visible in numbers or in physical characteristics. But I knew that I was different. There were certain expectations of me as a Greek-American girl that were unlike those of my American friends. For example, I had to attend the Greek language school each day after "American" school. But our extended family of Greek relatives gave me contact and support from more relatives than any of my friends could ever imagine. Over the years, I learned the skills of a homemaker and hostess for houseguests. I also became well aware that Greek girls were expected to marry Greek boys. I explained this to my American boyfriends, but they just didn't get it.

I was a slowly rising feminist. Although I didn't appreciate it at the time, having two older brothers and one younger one toughened me up. My Aunt Elaine says I am a survivor. Although my two older brothers and some of their friends demanded that I pretend to be their slave in their play and real worlds of King Fro and King Bobo (two kings, one slave), I was always searching for feminism and paid dearly for my revolts and mutiny in their escapades. But I must admit, I'm still trying to figure out how to transfer that stance of feminist-survivor to the male-dominated academic world. When I noted that I was a rising feminist living out my name, which means in Greek "the resurrected one," a male colleague assured me that I have arisen so I must be making progress.

I would talk back to boys who tried to bully me, and if they hit me I would hit them back, both at home and at school. I learned a lot of that from having three brothers who had many friends who visited our home every day. I was a tomboy and felt tough, or at least acted tough. In elementary school, I fought and kicked back at boys who bothered me at school until the principal said I would have to spend the whole recess holding a boy's hand walking around the playground with everyone watching. That stopped that, at least on a visible plane. There was a great part of me that was a rule-follower, but a rebellious part consistently surfaced. I remember questioning the rule for "only organized play allowed" in elementary school. We weren't allowed to just hang out and talk with one or two friends at recess. Who are the rules for anyway? In junior high, I wanted to talk to friends about schoolwork as well as social life. My teachers called me down for all of my efforts to collaborate and for my loud and articulate voice. I was becoming more and more aware of where authority lay in my life and in school. I spent a lot of time in my bedroom just thinking and writing.

My feminism gets played out in my teaching, research, and administrative work. I often ask, "Why can't I?" I am often proactive when I feel that an opportunity for change has come my way. For example, when I had to coordinate the first joint national and state accreditation visit in our state and realized that the process was still in the making, I took a proactive stance with others to design our university's visit (Samaras et al. 1999). We used a self-study model to structure the accreditation visit. Our institution used the planning for the visit as an opportunity to examine the education unit to assess the strengths of the program and the initiatives we had made and to determine what changes were necessary before the accreditors came to campus.

In another instance, I was excited to work with women scientists to evaluate a new environmental science program. I was even more excited when we found that female non-science majors, including early childhood and elementary education majors, preferred nontraditional teaching and evaluation measures in learning about science (Samaras, Howard, and Wende 2000). These new and exciting encounters with others pushed me to learn in stimulating ways. I was able to grow and develop by using relational knowing, which women do so well (Belenky, Clinchy, Goldberger, and Tarule 1986). I could not have done this kind of learning on my own. In 1999, I helped develop an interdisciplinary course with the major objective of teaching perspective-taking, which I share with you later. My early desire to collaborate and my nascent feminism have shaped my professional self in crucial ways; I am glad I stayed true to myself.

A ride down West Street takes me past the location of our family restaurant. The restaurant was about a 10-minute walk from our West Street home down a mixed business and residential street. My siblings and I were required to work at the restaurant; each of us contributed to what was good for the whole. It was what we did. Beginning at the age of 13, I worked as a busgirl and learned quickly to appreciate a hard-earned dollar in a very difficult business. I worked each shift and often had to cover for waitresses who couldn't or didn't make it to work, although for the most part the regulars were old-timers and were quite reliable. It taught me the importance of reliability and responsibility in the workplace. It also taught me that the situations of some people prevented them from working efficiently. One waitress was having chemotherapy. Another had a lousy husband who cheated on her, and another could never secure childcare. One stayed out too late drinking and had trouble with her boyfriends. I felt lucky that I was 13 and had a solid family. I try to remember these lessons when I work to teach students who won't cooperate with my methods.

As I walked to work at the restaurant, I would pass the only local newspaper company in town, liquor stores with flashing neon lights, a pharmacy, and low-income housing. I passed a bus station, a fire station, a few eating joints, an African-American church, a few bars, and some small businesses. Over time, I developed street smarts; I knew where and how to walk and how to look like I was cool even when I felt scared inside.

My biorhythms got very confused during the summertime, when each waitress took a week's vacation and I substituted for the various shifts. Having to wake up at 5:30 A.M. for the morning shift changed my lifestyle of staying out late. Working the late shift until 11:00 P.M. meant that I had to be careful of people who drank too much. I learned to be flexible, dependable, and alert to my surroundings. Over time, I became educated in how to waitress, take cash, "check out" the register, handle accounting, hostess, organize banquets, make the staff's weekly work schedule, and do any other duties I was assigned. As one waitress always used to say, "No use complaining." I learned to do whatever task I was given. This would be both a curse and a blessing in academia. I was amenable to learning and teaching anything, but it was a very long time before I learned to say no to unreasonable requests.

Our restaurant doors opened at 6:30 A.M. to serve a very regular crowd I came to know. There was a mix of business owners, mechanics, and blue-collar workers from nearby appliance stores; professionals from medical and law firms; and construction workers from local construction sites. I observed engineers scribbling concept webs on our napkins, politicians figuring out campaign funds on placemats, and other customers who had difficulty even reading the menu. During busy lunch hours, we served a hungry, hurried, no-nonsense crowd such as the clothing-store proprietors who needed to get back to their businesses a few doors away.

The restaurant was located near the Maryland State House, and it was also frequented by legislators, politicians, lobbyists, and lawyers. Around the block were various professional offices. I didn't enjoy some of the pushy regular clientele. At the restaurant, I learned that people who were well educated or had money weren't any better than those who had little education or were poor. I met a lot of rich smart people who weren't very nice. I recognized quickly that although some customers looked more important than others, they were not. The same can be said about the "level one" or "academically challenged" students I have taught, inner-city families I came to know through my work in schools, and people I have worked with in schools and universities.

My first teaching assignment was in 1970 as a volunteer teacher. I tutored a young child living in an urban renewal housing project area. I was studying for my undergraduate degree at the University of Maryland, College Park, where my fields were social studies and secondary education, with cognates in history and sociology. I have always been most curious to learn about society and how people think and develop. Social studies, history, sociology, psychology, and speech and drama were my favorite classes; I would later teach them all. My attraction to human development and developmental psychology followed easily from these interests.

In 1972, I took my first teaching job as a social studies teacher at Wiley H. Bates junior high school, the city's recently integrated school. I taught there for almost six years until I left after the birth of my first child. At one time, it was a school for African Americans, who were called "colored people" in the 1960s, or, if you were polite, "Negroes." I had a chance to teach in a largely middle-class white suburban high school where I student-taught, but I felt drawn to a city school and to challenges. In the 1930s, Wiley H. Bates, a successful African-American grocery store owner, had donated money toward the purchase of school-grounds for a public school for African Americans. The new high school opened in 1933. During the 1960s, some African-American children attended the "white" schools, but they were children of professionals. Wiley H. Bates High School was desegregated in 1966. Some whites were opposed to having their children attend the former school for blacks, but the transition was made, and parents of all colors who believed in the value of public education made it a successful place of learning.

While teaching, I completed a master's degree from The Institute for Child Study at The University of Maryland. When I received my master's degree in 1976 with my first child in utero, a male whom I had grown up with in the church community asked me in bewilderment, "What will you ever do with that advanced degree now that you are going to be a mother?" "I'll use it," I replied indignantly, although at the time I wasn't sure, either. It just seemed right for me.

In 1977, I went on a teaching leave from the public school for the birth of my first child and continued teaching human development courses in a cooperative university–school district project. I had the opportunity to work with teachers and counselors in student case study observation and analysis projects that they conducted in their schools. Their contextualized child observations made the class come alive. That experience was crucial to my decision to become a teacher educator; I realized that I could teach adults and that I enjoyed it. My compassionate friend Pat Mitchell encouraged me to continue to take more courses, and I enrolled in an early childhood curriculum course in 1978. I continued to learn because I enjoyed it.

During the 1980s, while taking courses and raising my children, I also taught part-time in preschools, in high schools, in a community college, and at four universities. Teaching became autotelic. I found I enjoyed teaching any age and any course. As an adjunct, I taught thirteen different college courses over a 15-year period, sometimes commuting between home and three universities within one semester. My traditional upbringing and understanding of young children's development told me to be student, mother, and teacher, and so I did them all, part-time and full-time. By my late 20s, I had exhausted myself; I suffered a severe bout of anemia that permanently discolored my skin.

My life as an unliberated female Greek-American would be both influenced and challenged by the women's movement. The most popular question asked women at dinner parties in those days was "What do you do?" "I am a mother and a doctoral student," I would reply. I noticed that if I mentioned my part-time teaching, people paid much closer attention to the conversation.

As I look back, I see how I often carried multiple roles and that I always carried the role of a woman-caretaker. First I was a young girl who was trained to be a hostess at our family parties and for the endless visitors who frequented our house. Because I was the oldest girl, I was responsible for my younger siblings and, later, my parents. As a young woman and waitress I learned to serve others and please the customer. It made me conscious and responsive, willingly and unwillingly, to the public, their demands, and their needs. Each role encouraged me to think about people's needs, especially those of my students.

I made note of how professors were teaching at the five colleges where I taught part-time. For the most part, little had changed from my college days. I looked at course syllabi, midterms, finals, and course structures. I heard lectures as I walked through hallways and conducted my own informal study. The professors who impressed me the most were those giving guest talks in each other's classes and conducting team research. In my college teaching, I began to experiment with devoting class time to dialogue with peer support and roundtable presentations.

How did I first learn about Vygotsky's work? I easily recall my doctoral studies during the 1980s with my doctoral advisor, Greta Fein. Under Greta's tutelage, I worked as a graduate research assistant on one of the first national studies to investigate the impact of computers on young children (Campbell and Fein 1986). My logged observations quickly became popular in the Department of Curriculum and Instruction for their telling nature, but I struggled to explain what I was able to see and understand in publishable language. My logs of pairs of young children working with different teachers on a computer in a university laboratory school unveiled the cognitive and affective potentials of computer usage (Wright and Samaras 1986).

When I looked at the logs more closely, I began to delineate the teacher's role in unleashing the potential of the children she was teaching. The timed logs indicated that the children stayed longer at the computer and were more constructively playful when the teacher gave suggestions and prompts rather than directives. This qualitative research appealed to me, although I was heavily trained as a quantitative researcher, which I used for my dissertation. When I explained my findings to my advisor, she directed me to look deeper into the works of Vygotsky, which were just becoming readily available in English at the time. I have been looking at them ever since.

Following some good hunches, I investigated and found that the teacher's mediation and scaffolded instruction, or instruction that was tailored to what children could achieve with gradations of support and with general and specific statements, were related to children's problem-solving, use of strategy, and self-regulation, or the ability to take greater responsibility for components of the task (Samaras 1991, 1996). Teaching 3-year-olds at the university laboratory preschool and later conducting floor training with teachers in Head Start programs in

Baltimore gave me firsthand experience in scaffolding the development of children and the professional development of inservice teachers. In 1990, I received my doctorate in curriculum and instruction/early childhood and teacher education after conducting research in sociodramatic play, children's problem-solving in the context of mediation by the teacher, developmental psychology, and teacher education.

When I became a teacher educator, I decided that if I was going to teach teachers how to create supports for children's learning, I should model that practice in my own classroom. Who was scaffolding preservice teachers' learning? Why weren't professors studying and reflecting the way they were asking their students to do? In Sumara and Carson's terminology (1997), I think ecologically; I believe that the way one lives one's life matters. I want to live and practice my profession with integrity and do something worthwhile for teachers and the children they teach.

❖ Chapter 2

A Platform for Change

Why are many preservice teachers not ready to teach and why don't they stay in the profession very long? Why will nearly half of all newly hired teachers leave the profession within their first five years? (Darling-Hammond 1997) Could it be related to the inadequacies of their course-work and field experiences? Researchers have criticized the "methods fetish" (Bartolome 1994; Macedo 1994) for breeding rigid routine rather than critical and reflective modes of thinking about planning and teaching. Some critics have suggested that what preservice teachers learn in methods courses perpetuates the status quo of traditional teaching practices; others suggest that their professors do not model the pedagogy they preach (Goodlad 1990; Levin 1990; Smith 1980).

What do preservice teachers learn in their education courses anyway? Should they themselves be learning in the way they are being taught to teach children—with subject matter content that is rigorous, with respect and care for their students, in active learning settings, and with support for self-regulation? Shouldn't we be analyzing teacher education programs and their outcomes? Shouldn't we be talking to the arts and sciences faculty who teach two-thirds of the other courses preservice teachers must take? How do the distribution and licensure courses in academic disciplines connect to the elementary school subjects they will soon teach?

Logbook, 21 April 1998

As I attended a national educational conference, a sense of déjà vu overcame me as I heard the rhetoric of performance-based accountability for teachers. I left the standing-room-only session and found a quiet sunny place to sit and reflect. I sank into a large overstuffed armchair and looked out the large tall windows dressed with satin valances. I casually skimmed through the conference program and again found the session titles—they were filled with words such as ACCOUNTABILITY, ASSESSMENT, and

ACHIEVEMENT. The words rang in my head like an alarm clock that I couldn't turn off or shut out. Trying to sort out the reform cries of numerous conference presenters I had heard earlier that day, I envisioned two trains. Although they appeared to be moving in a parallel direction, the destination of each train, or whether or not they would collide, was not clear.

In one train were teachers who had been teaching for a number of years and who had heavy workloads due to increased testing and demands for accountability. Many of those teachers would soon be leaving or retiring. Also in this first train were preservice and newly hired teachers, too many of whom would leave the profession shortly after they entered it. In the other train were politicians, business leaders, state school administrators, and the public sector. They were demanding a unified and systematic reform of higher professional and teaching standards, performance assessments of the content knowledge of teachers and students, and a rigorous and uniform three-tiered teacher licensing system.

The growing demand for teachers while the pool of qualified teachers diminishes and the justifiable initiatives for smaller classes, bonuses for teachers, higher pay, and mentors for beginning teachers each complicated the reforms. After all, economics and politics enter into school reform. As the train of teachers was quickly losing passengers at each stop, the other train was gaining passengers. For a brief moment, I saw myself boarding the second train as a reactor to the reform—perhaps I could begin methodically documenting preservice teachers' performance outcomes. Then my eyes caught the titles of the other sessions I had also been attending that day—they included the words SELF-STUDY. I said to myself, "I am an innovator." Will national standards enable educators to examine their own practice in an effort to improve students' performance? Will they allow educators to generate new knowledge from the bottom up to make instruction more effective?

Suddenly, my solitude was interrupted by a passing group of boisterous, well-dressed conference attendees who were laughing and talking about where they could go for a great lunch. I thought of the real world of the inner-city schools where I send my preservice teachers who have no idea of reform initiatives. I could not ignore the outside world of teaching as I taught inside the ivory tower. I must change the way preservice teachers are taught before they can change the way they teach. I have great respect for those that have contributed to inservice teachers' training, but better preservice preparation would be more efficient than prescriptive remedies after the fact.

My work context has provided me with an excellent platform for exploring a Vygotskian model. As an early childhood curriculum and instruction specialist, I work with early childhood and elementary preservice teachers in a deliberative and reflective teacher education program (Valli 1990). I use the word deliberative to mean a process that includes examining a dilemma from different points of view and a discussion of alternatives in order to decide on and assess the consequences of a particular course of action. I consider critical inquiry to be one of the best methods for continuous professional development. I feel at home in a department that values broad reflection and a creative search for solutions.

The CUA Reflective Teacher Model structures the development of preservice teachers' personal decision-making and action in dynamic teaching situations (see Figure 2.1). The framework serves as a tool to promote students' analyses of curriculum puzzlements that they encounter in teaching. Through inquiries into dilemmas found in practice, preservice teachers discuss actions and strategies that are based on professional knowledge, careful observation, and reflection. They are asked to consider the consequences, both positive and negative, of their actions. They write about dilemmas, multiple perspectives, and alternative action plans and are encouraged by faculty to consciously examine the consequences of their courses of action. During practicum and student teacher seminars, students make meaning of their individual observations through much dialogue with their peers and professors.

The framework provides a common language with which to converse and teach more critically and consciously. It incorporates the technical aspects of teaching with moral considerations and includes three elements of education: (1) commonplaces of the teaching situation; (2) dilemmas in teaching; and (3) reflective levels, or ways of thinking about the consequences of teaching decisions. Schwab's (1973) commonplaces of education are employed to help frame students' perspective-taking, or working to understand a situation from someone else's point of view (in this context, usually parents, students, or community members). Accordingly, every teaching situation has four components or commonplaces: (1) the teacher, or someone who instructs; (2) the student, or the learner; (3) the subject matter content, or knowledge, skills, values, attitudes, or ideas that are being presented and shared; and (4) the context, or the social milieu in which teaching occurs. In teacher preparation, context includes the ethos of the school and the classroom and the norms and expectations of students and teachers by the community and the broader society. The relations between the commonplaces are used as points for student reflection (Posner 1996; Schwab 1973) and to promote a relational analysis of the dimensions and problems of classroom life.

Dilemmas are another dimension of the framework that require preservice teachers to consider the multiple perspectives among the commonplaces (adapted from Berlak and Berlak 1981). Preservice teachers are asked to consider implications of three domains of dilemmas: (1) motivational or control dilemmas, or who should control what in education; (2) curriculum dilemmas, or issues related to knowledge, learning, students, and motivation; and (3) social dilemmas, or the context of the educational endeavor.

As preservice teachers implement their action plans, they are encouraged to consider a third dimension of the framework, van Manen's (1977) levels of reflection. The three levels of reflection are the technical, interpretive, and critical, which address the questions of how, what, and why, respectively. On a (1) technical level, preservice teachers consider how to approach and act on a dilemma located in practice. To promote reflective inquiry of their actions and empathetic understanding and what it might mean for others, preservice teachers are prompted to consider the (2) interpretive level of their decisions. They are asked to carefully deliberate the meaning of their actions and to consider the perspectives of learners and society. Foremost, they are encouraged to consider the (3) critical level of their choice, why they made the decision, and social justice issues. Their choice and action are not considered right or wrong but depend rather on their personal philosophy, the context, the subject matter, and student differences. They are asked to substantiate their position and consider its consequences.

Pedagogical preparation for elementary education majors includes early coursework in the introduction to teaching, foundations of education, human development, and the psychology of education. Field experiences are continuously and increasingly integrated with coursework throughout students' program of studies. Undergraduate and graduate-level preservice teachers are coached in a decision-making orientation toward teaching that is field based. The practicum and student teaching experiences require a continuous synthesis of coursework, review of the research, and integration of the conceptual framework in their field experiences. Once early childhood and elementary students are accepted into the teacher education program, they complete two professional semesters of methods courses taken concurrently with field experiences and a practicum seminar. Acceptance requirements include a

2.75 average in their education major, a 2.5 overall GPA, two letters of recommendation from education faculty, and passing scores on the Praxis I series.

Program Restructuring

Before I came to the university, program evaluations revealed that preservice teachers perceived the field experience as unconnected to their methods courses. Several problems had been identified through student evaluations. They had no situated learning or in-context planning experiences and had difficulty transferring skills learned in coursework to the real world of daily teaching. Preservice teachers participated independently of peers in a one-day-a-week yearlong practicum where they completed individual method course assignments for a hypothetical unit of instruction. Faculty observed that preservice teachers tended to identify with the school and the teacher in the classroom and were resistant to university assignments that were only hypothetical. The practicum field experiences did not promote critical and reflective thinking about individualized learning and teaching, opportunities for making curriculum decisions, the application of content knowledge, or a conceptualization of long-term planning. Consequently, many student teachers were unprepared for the student teaching experience.

In my first year at CUA it came to my immediate attention, as a student teacher supervisor, that student teachers had difficulty in long-term planning, particularly in seeing how individual lessons were linked to a unit of study. Teresa Lynn wrote in her final self-evaluation report:

> Long-term planning was a difficult aspect and so foreign, although it shouldn't be. You don't really know [how to plan a unit with lessons that have a meaning-ful sequence so learning is connected conceptually for students] until you're in the situation. [Then] you think about planning in a different way. You don't think of it as having to plan one lesson and then another one lesson. You think of it as, how am I going to do this unit?

Her cooperating teacher frequently expressed concern about her lack of readiness to "take over" the class. My evaluation notes indicated that the cooperating teacher infrequently shared her thinking about planning. She was particularly impatient about Teresa Lynn's developing planning skills. I also noted that the cooperating teacher did not offer the guidance and support in the areas that this student teacher needed. Although

Teresa Lynn had the potential to teach more efficiently and to plan more thoroughly, she was not clear about how to make her ideas work. She needed contingent support based on her responses to problems. Instead of receiving the gradated guidance she needed to learn how to infuse single lesson ideas into an existing curriculum, she was made to feel inadequate as a student teacher.

This tension that I observed often motivated me to think about how I could improve my teaching about planning. I went back to Vygotskian principles I learned during my doctoral work and discussed using a sociocultural stance with colleagues. First and foremost, I saw a need for more support from cooperating teachers and peers and formative assessment before the student teaching experience.

Logbook, 28 March 1993

I was driving down the road and saw a car bumper sticker that read "Rookie Driver." I said to myself, "Now that's a great way for others to know that this driver is new and might make errors in driving judgment." The driver is more than a "Student Driver," but still is not very experienced. I thought, "Maybe we should talk about rookie teachers instead of student teachers." After all, they are more than students now. They are each on the road to earning the title of teacher, but they aren't really ready. Is it fair to expect them to be? Student teachers are given rookie status, but like most rookie drivers, the short-term cram course is not enough to prepare them for the unpredictable roads ahead. Could practicum students be more like student teachers?

There was no structure in our existing practicum program for collective cognitive or social support in the field context from peers or cooperating teachers. Students had few opportunities to try out what they learned at the university and to see if any of it made a difference in their students' learning. Also, there was no connection between course assignments and readings and experience in the field. Although the problem had been identified, there was no structure for change. Nancy Taylor and I sketched out how the alignment of course and field might occur and then, working with school faculty, we took action (Samaras, Taylor, and Kelly 1994; Taylor, Samaras, and Gay 1994). It would be a critical point in my teaching and research and one where I would have an opportunity to act on my notions of a Vygotskian approach in preparing teachers as it aligned with the CUA Reflective Teacher Model and my belief in the self-study.

I conceptualized a framework for teacher educators' self-study so they too could reflect upon the commonplaces, dilemmas, and curriculum choices they make associated with teaching preservice teachers (see Figure 2.2). Like their students, teacher educators could also employ levels of reflection to consider the technical, interpretive, and critical consequences of their teaching decisions, particularly as they applied to Vygotskian notions. For example, on a technical level, if social and cultural influences shape development, what are some ways I could come to know my students' cultures? On an interpretive level, what might those efforts mean to my students' learning? On a critical and moral level, why do I believe that learning about my students is essential to teaching them? I discuss Vygotskian principles and my reflections on integrating them in my teaching in Part II.

Because our objectives were to align theory and practice with preservice teachers' self-study and reflection, two major changes occurred simultaneously—we restructured coursework and field experiences. Program restructuring for the early childhood and elementary programs began in 1992 and included the following program goals:

- provide preservice teachers with a coherent experience that will allow them to see the curriculum in action and the way learning experiences build upon learning experiences
- give preservice teachers an opportunity to design and carry out a sequence of instruction
- give preservice teachers an opportunity to learn instructional techniques from cooperating teachers and to try out practices advocated in coursework

In the restructured program, cohorts of early childhood and elementary education preservice teachers now complete two unique professional semesters with increased time and teaching responsibility in the field. Both professional semesters involve field experiences concurrent with methods coursework and practicum seminars. In the practicum seminars, preservice teachers are expected to share their reflections and communicate their thinking processes as they react to a specific problematic situation. This structure is to prepare them for an action research project that will be completed during the student teaching experience in which they will take action on a problematic classroom event.

During the first professional semester, preservice teachers take courses in children's literature, music in the elementary school, classroom management, and curriculum and instruction, which are carefully aligned with a two-half-days-a-week practicum at one of two schools. Preservice teachers work individually with students in small and large groups. The second professional semester involves methods courses in reading, mathematics, health and physical education, and social studies and science. Originally, the second professional semester field component included a three-half-days-a-week practicum. We changed this after two years largely because of scheduling conflicts with distribution course offerings, because of time and transportation factors, and because preservice teachers were not able to experience a complete teaching day or the subjects that were taught in the afternoon. Currently, the accompanying practicum is one half day and one full day per week. The two professional semesters allow all students to experience two different school contexts and to observe and participate in the opening and closing of a school year.

In addition to other teaching, I teach the curriculum and instruction course in the fall and the methods in social studies and science course in the spring. In my social studies and methods course, pairs of preservice teachers co-plan, teach, and evaluate an interdisciplinary unit. I have worked very closely with the university practicum liaison each semester and make it a point to visit cooperating teachers each semester. There have been program refinements, although I have consistently used the interdisciplinary unit project using Vygotskian pedagogy. An interdisciplinary unit is a strategy for teaching major concepts that links major ideas across disciplines while also teaching content, basic skills, and curriculum standards. I also encourage preservice teachers to integrate content from prior education courses and other methods courses to teach their students the connections that exist across disciplines so that children may construct knowledge in a meaningful manner.

I believe that learning occurs *during* the actual problem-solving and joint activity or shared tasks with others; for example, the exchange of interpersonal knowledge (or sharing between people) to enhance their intrapersonal knowledge (or knowledge that is internalized independently). The unit project gives preservice teachers a sense of ownership in their learning and a reason to experiment with what they are learning in coursework in a real setting. The unit assignments involve active reflection and a collective production of knowledge because students regularly discuss their observations, thinking, and teaching with their peers and cooperating teachers as they self-evaluate their work. A mutual goal, or shared task, creates a joint activity and a reason for dialogue, negotiation, and perspective-taking with peers and teachers.

The unit enables me to teach about the "big" ideas and long-term planning. It also creates the need to bring theory into practice right away. Preservice teachers need to understand such topics as school politics, classroom dynamics, structuring and managing daily activities, writing a lesson plan, pacing lessons, timing, sequencing, assessing through observation, and managing a classroom. Researching and integrating subjects suddenly has great significance. Preservice teachers need to know technique and subject matter, but these need to be integrated with and placed in the context of knowledge about their students and their students' reactions so they can make needed adjustments *during* their teaching. They then discover that the lesson plan must have fluidity and flexibility. They can't see that when they only write a lesson plan. They must do it. The integrated unit enables me to teach about three planning domains—pre-active, interactive, and post-active (Jackson 1968) —to support and assess their pedagogical and content knowledge.

The Interdisciplinary Unit

The unit, which centers on either a social studies or a science topic, is generated and negotiated from the existing classroom curriculum and the interest of the children. In their concept-based units, preservice teachers develop lessons that teach about such concepts as universality, multiculturalism, diversity, and the environment (see Jarchow, Midkiff, and Pickert 1998 for some outstanding lesson samples related to global and social studies education created by my students).

Preservice teachers are paired in the same classroom and work together on the unit throughout the entire semester while receiving guidance from peers, cooperating teachers, and university professors. Using e-mail has expedited the feedback. Professors who are teaching other methods courses also use the unit as a place to contextualize their assignments and for preservice teachers to demonstrate their knowledge of course concepts. For example, in their reading methods course, preservice teachers are required to develop an annotated bibliography of children's books used in the unit and to enact a qualitative analysis of students' reading performances in their practicum classroom. In the mathematics methods course, preservice teachers plan and conduct a problem-solving lesson. Preservice teachers in the health and physical education methods course have planned for movement experiences to teach social studies and science concepts.

Each assignment in the social studies and science methods course entails both technical and reflective components. For example, during the pre-active phase of planning, preservice teachers research background information about their unit topic and discuss the rationale they used in selecting content; the rationale must include consideration of children's developmental needs. According to Shulman (1987), content knowledge is an essential component of the knowledge base of teaching. As subject generalists, however, it is difficult to be an expert in all subjects. Accordingly, preservice teachers are assigned to research and write a background knowledge paper so they recognize that they can and must learn content before teaching it. The fact that they will be teaching the material shortly motivates them to master it.

I also introduce concept mapping so that preservice teachers can demonstrate their pre-planning conceptions and post-planning conceptions of the subject content of the unit (Novak and Gowan 1984). This allows me to guide and assess their content knowledge before and after research, and it allows them to visualize and demonstrate the conceptual connections of the topic of their unit. In turn, concept mapping is an evaluation tool they can choose to use to measure their students' understanding before and after implementation of the unit. The background knowledge paper is submitted early in the semester so preservice teachers can begin unit planning. However, the topic is continually researched as new questions surface from the questions and interests of the children.

The Author's Chair is one pre-active planning assignment I designed. Writers present their own writing to peers, who may then ask questions of the author. The cooperative search is another partnered assignment in which pairs investigate and share personal planning questions generated from their interests and the experiences they have in the practicum (e.g., In what ways can I use local art museums in my unit on China? How do I design an equitable science fair?). As the semester unfolds, another pre-active planning assignment is a field-trip lesson that is connected to the unit. Preservice teachers actually walk through their trip before implementation, examining safety issues, checking whether the site is suitable for their students, making arrangements, acquiring permission, setting the time, and so forth—an extremely technical and essential part of planning for thirty elementary-age children riding a metro rail! I encourage them to use the rich museum resources in Washington, D.C.; many museums in the city require no entrance fee. Additionally, a reflective evaluation of the field trip is completed in terms of Schwab's (1973) four commonplaces: teacher, student, subject matter, and context. A science shadow assignment, adapted from Carol Livingston's science teaching, is a pre-active assignment that is specifically focused on science content and pedagogy. In pairs, preservice teachers shadow, interview, and analyze science teachers' thinking about planning before, during, and after a science investigation lesson. Each writes and compares their observations and shares it with the class.

During the interactive phase of planning, preservice teachers implement their lessons in the field and then talk about their experiences during the practicum seminar. During practicum seminars, preservice teachers read their reflective journal entries of dilemmas encountered while implementing the unit (e.g., adjusting teaching to reach all children, overlapping skills when discipline problems arose while teaching, finding out that first-graders ask sophisticated questions, what it's like to discuss the Civil War as a Caucasian teacher in a class of all African-American students). Other class projects that provide an audience for learning include participating in roundtables about science principles and sharing post-planning concept maps of background knowledge. There are opportunities for peers to provide coaching for lessons implemented in the field, to give oral critiques of field-trip sites, to offer analyses of science shadow experiences, and to present the results of cooperative searches.

These peer-assisted collaborative learning activities are used to foster metacognitive thinking about teaching and reflection about actual classroom situations through dialogue. They also facilitate collegial interaction and counteract the status quo of isolation for new teachers. As Pugach and Johnson (1990) note, peer collaboration with reflection can involve clarifying and reframing problems with others, summarizing, generating solutions, and considering the consequences of one's actions. These reflective skills will be useful to preservice teachers later during their student teaching experience when they conduct an action research project and when they become a teacher. Preservice teachers adopt a "partnership perspective" (Erdman 1983) as they develop, discuss, experiment, and reflect on their lessons with peers and cooperating teachers. Preservice teachers meet in a three-way mid-term evaluation conference with their cooperating teachers and university liaison. They continuously receive opportunities to analyze, evaluate, and reconstruct their experiences with planning and to discuss what they learned in their own words.

The last section of the unit requires a final assessment of the unit and reflection; preservice teachers write about what they have learned and discuss whether their students acquired the concepts and skills they were teaching, what they would do differently, and how the unit project reflects their philosophy of what it means to be a teacher. In a videotaped poster session, preservice teachers present pre-planning and post-planning maps of unit planning and discuss their metacognitive notions of how to plan the unit; this is accompanied by a written paper. In a progress report of their fieldwork, as outlined by Posner (1996), preservice teachers describe the context of their field experience, the goals they set for the practicum experience, what they learned from the field experience, learning episodes they observed, the generalizability of field observations, ways in which they achieved their goals, and future goals. They meet again for an end-of-semester evaluation conference with their cooperating teacher and university liaison.

During our last class, I hold a debriefing session in which we collectively discuss our reconstruction of experiences (e.g., by creating class webs, writing a letter to the next cohort, outlining course themes, etc.). A privately scheduled audiotaped exit conference is conducted with each preservice teacher and myself. A written self-evaluation paper is required that discusses the quality of their work, participation, and effort for the semester; how the student currently views him or herself as a teacher; how they arrived at the insights they describe; and future professional goals. I talk about these course assignments later in more detail in Part II.

While I worked with colleagues on research in preparation for restructuring the program in projects such as studying former student teachers' beliefs about and experiences of reading and language arts instruction, I also conducted a self-study of the Vygotskian pedagogy I employed. My steadfast research and practices as well as discussions about its value allowed it to become more and more central to our restructuring efforts. I insisted on studying the impact of contextualized learning that includes formative assessments of preservice teachers' thinking about planning. I reflected on this often. Below is a note to a colleague:

Logbook, 10 October 1994

We ask our students to hang in there, and we ask a lot of them. Although preservice teachers are well versed in writing lesson objectives, gathering activities, and testing new knowledge, little attention has been given to the development of their notions of planning for the big picture.

They have not constructed a clear representation of the larger frame. Offering text guides and taxonomies of objectives is decontextualized and promotes a categorical perspective of learning for teachers and students alike.

Real opportunities for planning arrive with the student- teaching experience, where students' experimentation and true authorship is penalized through the evaluative and intimidating nature of that experience. Assessments made while learning to teach, instead of evaluations made of teaching, may better contribute to preservice teachers' broadened conceptions of long-term planning. The dynamics of talking about planning in the pre-active, interactive, and post-active phases may be the conduit for meaningful learning experiences.

The planning of the unit helps anchor a lot of teaching components that preservice teachers have learned about—planning, teaching reading, taking a field trip, doing a science investigation lesson, and handling a classroom—all at the same time. Better yet, it's theirs. They own the unit and reflect on it constantly (I think). It's small but essential to their coursework and conceptualization about planning beyond the one-day lesson. Can/will the interviews we conducted tell us this?

Over the years, I kept files of each cohort's work and my field notes and questions. One of the most interesting research questions to me was "How do preservice teachers develop an understanding of planning the unit?" At the end of the semester, they share their reflections in a paper that illustrates the metacognitive process of how they learned to plan, including pre-planning and post-planning concept maps of their notions about unit planning. In the paper assignment, students explain the development of their planning—how they attempted to integrate factual and conceptual knowledge; what kind of support they received from peers, professors, and cooperating teachers in that process; their greatest struggle; the small and large planning problems they encountered; and advice to future classmates from the lessons they learned.

As I returned to the data to look at the issue of planning more closely, I found that the structure of the unit promoted preservice teachers' discourse about and reflection on pre-active, interactive, and post-active planning. Self-reporting by preservice teachers indicated that although they had to deal with their own survival needs as novices, they were aware of and concerned about individualizing learning and student outcomes and tried to adapt lessons to the diverse needs of their students. They were able to observe and recognize the impact of their teaching, which is surprising in light of the research that argues that only more "expert" teachers develop decision-making skills and the ability to make the curriculum their own (Bendixen-Noe and Redick 1995; Westerman 1991).

Being prepared to teach meant they had to continue to research and locate information about what they were teaching as well as direct students to sources of information. Over time, preservice teachers were able to witness the impact of their teaching on their students' learning and learned to make adjustments in their teaching as needed. The classroom dynamics gave them opportunities to address questions related to curriculum issues, such as, What is the fit between what I want to teach, the existing classroom curriculum, and what students need to know for standardized tests? The environment of a particular grade and class allowed them to test their teaching theories. They learned about the details and scope of teaching by trying out strategies they were currently learning about in their methods courses. It was not just that lessons here and there were required from different professors; the lessons were implemented in real-life situations. The practicum gave them a sense of what the classroom is like and a more realistic approach to teaching. (Samaras 2000b).

The shape of the restructuring changed as I listened seriously to preservice teachers' comments each semester about what they felt was working and what they felt needed to be changed. In the first years, some students were paired and others were not. This was sometimes because we found some cooperating teachers who were interested in pairing and sometimes because the number of students was unequal. The unpaired ones, who were typically the graduate students, felt they were disadvantaged. Laura stated, "Either pair all of us or none of us." She was right. They were all novice teachers. The pairing was to help preservice teachers experiment with co-teaching and a collegial model for the professional development of teachers. We moved away from using schools that weren't interested in the pairing arrangement. Some schools had small classrooms with two co-teachers already in each room. When there are unequal numbers of preservice teachers, we encourage the preservice teacher and cooperating teacher to be the pair. Ideally, there is actually a triad of partners in a contexualized learning experience—peer with peer and each preservice teacher with the cooperating teacher. Depending on the personalities, social skills, and negotiating skills of the participants and the mentoring skills of the cooperating teacher, some preservice teachers establish strong bonds with each other while the cooperating teacher serves as an auxiliary support. Others work as a team of three with the cooperating teacher as either an equal or an expert, and a few have worked less with each other and more with the cooperating teacher. At any rate, structures for support are built into the model; some preservice teachers use them more than others.

Another major shift in the restructuring occurred after researching the instructional role of the mentorship the cooperating teachers provided for our preservice teachers. Originally, we were examining the global effects of program changes, but I kept thinking back to my supervision of Teresa Lynn, who didn't have a supportive cooperating teacher or a chance to learn about long-term planning. If the practicum experience is the forerunner that prepares students for student teaching, then what difference does it make in their understanding of teaching and how does that happen?

Logbook, 29 October 1994
    I think the research begs the question of how this new practicum format prepares preservice teachers for student teaching. Or does it? What can make it better? I don't want to just say it is an extended practicum. There's something more powerful than that going on. If one of our goals is to give preservice teachers an opportunity to learn instructional techniques from cooperating teachers and to try practices that are advocated in coursework, perhaps they need more scaffolding from the cooperating teacher. Just situating learning with free rein, particularly without peer help or maturity on the preservice teacher's part, is not productive. This goes back to my thinking about the need to provide a "good" and supportive model, or a cooperating teacher who allows them to learn to teach while teaching, works within their zones of proximal development, and knows when to let them try things alone.

With these issues in mind, I returned to audiotaped interviews that we had conducted with cooperating teachers but had never analyzed. I asked the university practicum liaison, Shelly Gismondi, then a doctoral candidate in administration and policy studies, to join me in analyzing this data. Shelly visited the practicum schools weekly to observe and support our students in their field placements. She also conducted three-way conferences with each preservice teacher and cooperating teacher and quickly relayed to me any red flags she observed. After researching the role of the cooperating teacher, we found two unusual cases that were outliers, or teachers who stood out from others. They characterized each end of the spectrum of structuring support for the preservice teacher (Samaras and Gismondi 1998).

Preservice teachers' cognition is placed within the activity of the participants within a particular context. Of course, both the quality of support from the cooperating teacher and the context for preservice teachers' learning are important, but we also discovered that when the support from the cooperating teacher is not adequate, the peer scaffolder becomes paramount. This research is now shared with cooperating teachers as we explain our program and ask them to do the great service of inviting our students into their teaching and classrooms. Our findings about the supportive process are discussed in detail in Chapter 7.

A recent shift I have made in my teaching is to clearly announce to preservice teachers that they must be proactive innovators within standards-driven curriculums (Samaras 2000a). We are teaching in a time of mandated state and national standards, national tests, and demands for uniformity. Although our program philosophy promotes an emergent curriculum that develops out of students' interests, it is becoming increasingly challenging to enact such a curriculum as state and national officials call for prescribed curriculum outcomes. As the social context has changed, I have asked preservice teachers to find innovative ways to incorporate students' interests into the written curriculum. For example, in a unit on Washington, D.C., I ask them to find out what students want to know about their community, then integrate the answers with the topics they are required to "cover." The curriculum will still belong to us if we don't give up. Otherwise we are victims. Looking at who I am and how I teach helped me to push aside preconceived and traditional notions of teaching and focus on innovation.

In the next section, I offer a discussion of four Vygotskian principles as they apply to my ways of teaching preservice teachers. I have found the following Vygotskian principles most relevant to how I teach: (1) social and cultural influences shape development; (2) learning occurs during situated and joint activity; (3) cognition is always socially mediated, especially through language; and (4) education leads development. I place descriptions of course strategies, assignments, and field projects within a theoretical explanation of each Vygotskian principle. In addition to discussing the ways I teach, I offer an explanation of why I believe each principle is useful to preservice teachers. Reflections of my education-related life history are intertwined with this discussion. I present the strategies as examples, not recipes, of what I have found to be useful. They are not *the* way, or the only way, to integrate these principles, and they have been refined over time. I have yet to discover other ways.

Part II. Synergy: Who I Am and How I Teach

❖Chapter 3
Knowing Students

Vygotskian Principle 1.
Social and cultural influences shape development.

Logbook, 23 January 1997

I have met many principals during my years in education. When I meet many of them, I can feel their energy in trying to improve children's learning. They work very hard. I also sense their feeling of urgency and the pressure from school boards and parents to improve school test scores. I discern that regardless of which curriculum model they use, the most successful principals are ones who know how to personalize instruction. They often talk of building a team or working for each child by giving every child an opportunity to learn.

When one principal introduced her elementary school to me today, she remarked that each child has a story that teachers need to know and try to understand in order to teach them. Why should that be any different for my students who are preservice teachers? Who are my students—really? What are their stories? How have their backgrounds helped shape their thinking about how schools should be organized or how students should be taught? What will they be like as teachers?

Vygotsky spoke of a sociocultural approach because he believed that social and cultural influences shape the development of children. He viewed cognition as a social phenomenon. According to Cole and Scribner (1978), Vygotsky was the first modern psychologist to argue that culture becomes a part of each person's nature. Thought arises through the individual's absorption of social experience in historical spaces (Popkewitz 1999). Individual learning and development are connected to the social and cultural world in which individuals grow.

Believing in the potential of individual children and that there were no universal stages of development, Vygotsky advocated that teachers needed to diagnose and mediate students' learning rather than use standardized tests to assess them. This interaction could lead the learner toward higher-level processes, which would, in turn, produce changes in the learner's nature. Since a child's social experiences influence the way he or she thinks about and interprets the world, the child's historical and cultural setting should be integral to the educational methods.

Self-Study Reflection

Greek-American values include the importance of family, education, church, ethnic pride, the work ethic, "philoxenía," or friendship to strangers, and "philótimo," or respect for oneself and consequently others (Rouvelas 1993). Unlike the Greeks who came after World War II, my parents believed in the ideals of the Horatio Alger era as well as the customs and values that the people who came in the 1920s and 1930s brought to America (see Moskos 1989). In many ways, those homespun values brought here from the small Greek villages have been instilled in me. It's as if they were frozen in time. I emerged out of the immigrants' experience with my parents' ideals of hard work, perseverance, and energy of will as my strength. I remember when I explained to one of my education professors that I had worked a long time to reshape my B-minus research paper. She chuckled when I told her I was a hard worker. She really didn't take time to understand how that notion was so central to my being.

Cultural and social contexts affect preservice teachers' perceptions of both themselves and the potential of their students. I use self-study strategies with preservice teachers so they can hold a mirror before their biases and think about how those biases impact what and how they teach. This enables them to acknowledge that each student also has a story placed in his or her own unique upbringing, historical space, and culture. It also allows me to frame examples around their experiences in order to pique their interest and arouse their curiosity as I teach them. Our perspectives are influenced by our backgrounds, experiences, and culture. Individual learning and development are connected to the social and cultural world in which individuals grow. I reflect on how that principle applied to my life experiences and about the significance of my sociocultural perspective in light of my early experiences at the restaurant our family owned for thirty years, The Royal.

Self-Study Reflection

The Greeks who own restaurants are the lucky ones. Restaurants can teach so much about people, character, and life's challenges. I was taught and lived the American work ethic, the immigrant's dream of success. I was taught to respect the hand that feeds me. At the restaurant I learned that relationships and responsiveness to others are what sustain us during our difficulties, regardless of who we are. I learned many life skills and a great deal about working with others who were our "restaurant help."

I look fondly on my learning experiences with the waitresses and head cook, who I shall call Mr. Charles, an African American. It didn't matter how well he read, or if he read at all. He could really cook. We had a connection through our shared activity of getting food to the customers and preparing the menu. I wrote down the next day's lunch and dinner specials that Mr. Charles dictated to me, then I would type them up and run them off on the messy, make-no-mistake mimeograph machine. My friend Judy reminds me how I complained about that black mimeograph ink that stained the skin under and around my fingernails—a teenage girl's nightmare!

After lunch hour, Mr. Charles and I would snap string beans together on the large wooden chopping block in the big restaurant kitchen while we chatted about how to make rice pudding for sixty people using handfuls and finger pinches as measurements. He taught me about American food words like yams and succotash, which were not familiar foods to us. He listened to me practice on the piano in the basement banquet room while he rested between the breakfast and lunch shifts and insisted that I wasn't bothering him, but of course I was.

It puzzled me that Mr. Charles typically came in the back kitchen door instead of through the front door past the customers. The younger African-American and Caucasian staff did not. He looked so uncomfortable the few times I saw him scurry through the front door of the restaurant with his eyes cast downward, his dressy cap pulled low, covering much of his face. He would give a brief nonverbal greeting to me as he passed. Mr. Charles was a gentleman and always worked hard. I watched how angry my father got when a Caucasian cook came out of the kitchen after lunch hour and talked to the customers in his meat-stained apron instead of working. I observed a lot about race, class, power, and status through the behavior of our customers. I mentally recorded the inequalities I observed. My restaurant associations would influence my decision to teach at a newly integrated junior high school instead of at the suburban high school I was invited to teach at in 1972.

The diversity of my associations at the restaurant helped me see that although we are not all the same, every human is worthy of respect. I believe that a sensitivity to and knowledge of what people bring to a teacher-learner encounter makes teaching easier. Teacher educators can become more aware of the issues preservice teachers bring to their teaching and the curriculum choices they might make. For example, if a preservice teacher has received twelve years of schooling in a suburban private school with a fairly homogeneous population, he or she may experience some culture shock teaching in an urban setting such as in the District of Columbia public schools. A preservice teacher may dislike gifted and talented students because she was mislabeled a "slow learner" and was taunted by the "smart" students.

One of the best gifts you can give students is to listen with your full attention to what they say verbally and nonverbally. I often ask myself, "Do I speak so that I can say what I want to say and cover, or do I speak to communicate something my students can relate to and that matters to them?" I try to listen better to become aware of how long it takes, or how hard it is, for some of them to see the gestalt, or the patterns and the connections between the details and concepts that order them. In contrast to the way it was during my earlier years of teaching, today my students freely share their learning disabilities with me, although I have to look beyond the labels to see their struggles and their strengths.

Throughout my teaching, I have always found that one of the most powerful factors that influences my students' learning is to let them know that I care about them and that I am trying to know them. Respect and the ethic of care are keys to effective teaching (Noddings 1992; Mayeroff 1971). I believe that caring for my students also encourages the best in myself. Collinson (1999) speaks of the need for teacher-student relationships and student-student relationships in educational reform. I have purposely structured and researched both the affective and cognitive support structures for preservice teachers so that my students can come to know each other better and think about the social and cultural influences that have shaped their development (Samaras 1998b).

I ask my students how they decided to become teachers and discover that life circumstances have impacted each student differently. Sophia watched her younger sister treated unfairly as a special education student and wants to give all children an opportunity to learn. Anna Noel was the oldest of eleven children; she has enjoyed teaching her siblings. Elizabeth has worked as a children's nurse and wants to work with "healthy" children and have the summers off. (She later discovered that teaching doesn't change either of those situations.) Christa, a former engineering student, informed her parents that she really always wanted to teach. Tom learned in a climate of fear in a strict and orderly school environment and is hesitant to try cooperative learning strategies in his teaching. Jessie's high school mathematics teacher discriminated against her because she had to leave his classroom to pursue more advanced studies. What each of these stories suggests is that forces have influenced preservice teachers' development that may offer clues to how to teach them more effectively.

I let my students know that I care about what matters to them, and I try to incorporate their interests in my teaching. I recall the time we discussed teaching styles and the use of formative feedback. I asked Magdalene, a college basketball player, to take our class outdoors to teach us how to block a player while the class took notes on her feedback statements.

Ways of Knowing Students

Today, the value I place on knowing the social and cultural influences that have shaped the development of my students gets played out in my pedagogy in multiple ways. These efforts are generally supported in the larger milieu of the Catholic institution where I work. I teach the same cohort of early childhood and elementary preservice teachers for one year. In the first professional semester, I teach a curriculum and instruction course, and in the second, I teach a course in methods of teaching social studies and science. This arrangement of teaching the same preservice teachers for one year incorporates Vygotsky's emphasis on personal history and the importance of understanding the development of preservice teachers' social interactions and relationships over time. The Reggio Emilia system uses these principles to great effect (Berk and Winsler 1995, 145). Additionally, my positions as director of teacher education and coordinator of academic advising enable me to meet many of the preservice teachers, and sometimes their families, before I teach them.

Throughout our year together, I use several strategies to know my students. I come a little closer to understanding what preservice teachers do and do not understand about teaching and subject matter through assignments such as their pre-planning and post-planning concept maps of unit planning and knowledge of their unit topic. Extensive and ongoing opportunities for self-study and self-evaluation, narratives of professional growth, metacognitive traces of unit planning, and audio-taped interviews allow me to see who they are becoming as teachers. Here, I share just a few of my ways of knowing: educated-related life histories, diverse contexts for viewing self in relation to others, professional growth papers, critical episodes in learning, and exit conferences and interviews.

Education-Related Life History Assignment

I have found that when I try to consider the perspectives of others it helps me see the aspects of a problem that go beyond my own needs. This is no easy task, but it is made easier by listening to the stories students can tell us. I explain to my students how my three children remind me of my intermittently dogmatic attitude of not listening carefully enough to the points of view of others. They force me to view children's development firsthand with their lively perspectives on life. It's fun to pretend to be queen, but they keep me straight about my sometime desire to be the only voice in family matters. My husband also reminds me that my perception of a situation is not always the way he sees it. My drama work in conflict resolution has also made me more aware of the points of view of others, to engage in perspective-taking. Cultivating this awareness is a lifelong task.

Once my students and I begin to trust each other, we talk about their past schooling experiences. I ask my students to place their energies in the present, absorbing and savoring it, while they try to sort out their past in relation to their notions of teaching and schooling. Impressed by the work of Bullough (1994a; 1994b) and Cole and Knowles (1995) on education-related life history approaches, I have adapted it in my teaching. I ask my students to describe the most positive and negative experiences in their schooling and how they think critical events and people have affected their teaching. Why? According to Vygotsky, development can be understood as the internalization of social activities. Past interactions and relationships with our culture—our teachers, peers, families, and communities—can tell us much about ourselves.

I enthusiastically read preservice teachers' education life histories. I attempt to understand their interests; for example, why certain students are interested in doing their action research paper on shy children, on children who were teased, or on heterogeneous classrooms. My hope is that this activity will encourage them to begin to look more carefully at the students entrusted to them. We all have issues, and life gives us the chance to work them out so we can appreciate our work better.

Self-Study Reflection

At our West Street home, I would rise in the morning and look out the window that faced our backyard, praying to God for a swimming pool. Eventually, when I was 14 years old, my father constructed a wading pool from the foundation of an old pond he found in our yard. My sister Alexis, who is ten years younger than I, often played in the pool. When the pool was empty, my brothers would pitch pennies toward its drain with their gangs of friends. I wondered what I had done wrong not to get my pool and instead to have one that only came up to my knees! I finally decided that I never told God what size the pool should be or when it should arrive. I share this amusing story with preservice teachers when I explain to them the need for well-detailed lesson plans. Be specific! God has lots of requests. We laugh together, and it feels good, because I have revealed a part of myself to them. Very slowly, an unspoken trust develops. We promise not to laugh *at* each other no matter what stories we tell. This will prove important when they share their first lessons.

I first experienced what I try to teach my students by writing about my own education-related life history (Samaras 1995). Because of the openness I ask of my students, I begin with my own snapshots of schooling and perspectives on learning in the hope that they will feel comfortable when they share theirs with our class. This is similar to what psychoanalysts are required to do when they go through analysis in order to understand what it is like to be analyzed. Because I have studied my own education-related past, I have a basis from which to understand that my students also come from cultures that have shaped them. I recognize that how they were taught will influence how they will teach, both positively and negatively. The negative experiences are the greatest teachers if preservice teachers can recognize and learn from them. At the least, they have an opportunity to reflect on the effects of past issues on their teaching.

Self-Study Reflection

I played endlessly at make-believe under our large, dying weeping willow tree or on the jungle gym where I performed increasingly difficult stunts. Playing make-believe taught me the power of using my imagination as I escaped to exotic lands in my play. Practicing on the bar of the jungle gym taught me to take risks and to feel good about my talents. I think I would have had a high score on a kinesthetic knowledge scale, but body intelligence wasn't a hot topic in those days, especially for females. My ninth-grade career search indicated that I should be a physical education teacher, but I heard that there were really hard science courses you had to take, so in the absence of any guidance, I didn't pursue it. I would first learn to swim and take modern dance classes at the age of 28 after the birth of my second child.

After I give some highlights of my education-related life history, preservice teachers present their stories in small groups and share them with their cooperating teachers. We then have a class analysis of education-related life history themes. Preservice teachers often comment that they strive to have the opposite teaching characteristics of their "awful" teachers. I wonder about the degree of self-regulatory learning they have experienced in their own schooling. They remember little things like being allowed to use erasable pens for the first time or not having to raise their hands to sharpen their pencils or getting permission to go to the bathroom. I think about the directive teaching style many have experienced in their schooling. Others talk about feeling stupid, bored, challenged, and inferior.

In an education-related life history, Jason wrote about how one teacher determined levels of reading ability:

> The teacher went about this by having a spelling bee. Whoever had the most words correctly spelled was placed into the upper-level workbooks. I had only three misspelled words and thus was placed in the upper-level workbook. As it turned out, the workbook had nothing to do with spelling words. As the first week went by, I experienced great difficulty with the workbooks. As a result, my English teacher placed me down to the lower-level English workbook. This was devastating to me because I felt that I was stupid. It lowered my self-esteem.

Jason also writes about a teacher who stayed after school to help him with whatever he needed. "What he did for me is what I do for students. I want students to feel a sense of trust with me." When they work in classrooms, I ask them to again reflect on their education-related pasts. June, a preservice student who considered herself an average student when younger, remarked:

It seems like this teacher is losing a lot of her average students by not challenging them. The brightest and the weakest students seem to get all the attention. So I often side with the average students and pair them with students who understand the material. I say, "Why don't you help each other?" I always say to them, "Make sure you help her. Is she doing alright? Do you think this is right? What do you think she needs?" Because I know that when I was a student, I was wonderful in some subjects and not wonderful in others. I knew I was only an average student in math, and the whole class knew it.

Below is the assignment I give my students:

We will begin the semester by looking back into your education-related past. You are asked to write an education-related life history and share it with your cooperating teacher and our class. Use the subheadings below as guidelines:

- **Personal school experiences:** Consider your experiences of school, how school felt, and how you best learned and when you felt most valued, connected, and at peace, or least valued, most disconnected, and at war with yourself and with school. What are the images you see? What metaphors come to mind?

- **Important people and events:** Identify important people and events that significantly influenced your decision and your thinking about teaching and how they influenced you.

- **Current philosophy and goals as teacher:** Again weave this discussion back to early influences as they apply.
  Consider:
  I learn best when...
  My role as a teacher is to...
  The goal of education should be...
  By the end of the year, I hope my students will...
  The purpose of evaluating my students is...

After writing your life history, read Lortie, D. (1975). *School teacher: A sociological study*. Chicago: University of Chicago Press. Be prepared to share your writings in a monologue presentation of your education-related life history to our class. Grading criteria include coverage of each subheading, depth of retrospective reflection, language conventions, and class presentation (adapted from Bullough 1994a).

Diverse Contexts for
Viewing Self in Relation to Others

Self-Study Reflection

I walked in two worlds as I struggled to find my own place and balance. I was proud to learn about my heritage when I studied ancient Greece, which I learned about in American and Greek school. I couldn't participate in after-school activities because I had to rush home to go to Greek school, which I attended each afternoon through junior high school. My English linguistics skills were not as fully developed as those of my friends. I was often embarrassed when I did not know American clichés and idioms that I did not learn at home.

Many of our future teachers do not have life experiences that will prepare them for the diverse cultures of the students in today's classrooms. The education-related life histories of my students often reveal that many of them have attended small suburban middle- to upper-class Catholic elementary and high schools with relatively homogeneous populations. The parochialism phenomenon is not particular to our university. Future teachers will also be of similar profiles; the typical teacher of the future will be a white female from a small or suburban community who will most likely return to teach middle-income children (The American Association of Colleges for Teacher Education 1990; Garibaldi 1992). Unfortunately, most preservice teachers cannot comprehend the cultural and educational needs of the majority of the students in America's classrooms.

Many of the graduates at CUA choose to teach in high-poverty urban schools, especially in the District of Columbia. But most don't stay long. The faculty at CUA has found that although the school culture may be quite different from their own, the reason they leave the schools is largely because they become discouraged because of the lack of administrative or mentoring support (Taylor and Wilson 1997). I tell my students about my own experience as a young teacher. In my first teaching job, I worked with "challenging" junior high school students. Some of the African-American 13- and 15-year-olds said that I didn't understand them because I was white. Sometimes I cried privately at home. At CUA, we work to prepare our student teachers to teach in classrooms with diverse populations. We also offer peer mentoring experiences.

Beginning in their freshman year, preservice teachers gain teaching experience in urban, public, or Catholic elementary schools with diverse populations and submit weekly journals of their reflections. They work in a variety of schools; not all of them are model settings, but they expose them to the consequences of school and community contexts, curriculum models, and parental influences. Additionally, the multiple placements offer them a viewpoint of how social and cultural issues might have shaped the development of their students. I trust that preservice teachers leave us with a better sense of who they are and the beauty of our pluralism. Here's a fascinating journal entry by Janet, a Caucasian preservice teacher who was completing her practicum in a school of 100 percent African-American students:

> My teacher asked me if I would mind going across the hall to speak with the other fourth-grade teacher's class. The day before, her class had a heated discussion about races, prejudices and "white" people. This first-year teacher was disturbed and thought her class had never encountered a white person before. She asked if I would speak about myself, my hobbies. I was very nervous to stand in front of this class and talk about myself. So many questions were running through my head. Was I going to be a good example?
>
> I ended up speaking to the class for an hour. They asked me a lot of questions and were really surprised by my answers. Some were amusing questions typical fourth-graders ask. Someone asked if I really was white. Another asked if I only listen to country music. I think they were really surprised that I had more in common with them then they had thought in the beginning. If it truly was the first time some of these children had a conversation with a white person, I am confident that I made an impression on them…It was a truly amazing experience. I can't really explain how I felt in front of that class. It gave me tremendous confidence and joy to see that I made an impact on these children. I know that throughout my years growing up, I have been surrounded by an incredible amount of prejudices. I grew up in a very white neighborhood and attended an all-white school. It was so great for me to have the situation reversed—to see the opinions and feelings firsthand.

Here's one of my favorite journal entries. This insightful preservice teacher is trying to know her students, to know what they are learning and not learning. Sallie has a new awareness of the problematic nature of designated months to honor diversity. She wrote:

> February is Black History Month and this school is making a genuine attempt to address the history of Black Americans. However, I found the implementation to be shallow. The teacher passes out a worksheet and reads a few paragraphs about the day's historical figure and then the students either color in their picture or

complete provided activities using words that refer to this person. As I walked around the room over the course of the first week, I found that students were missing the point entirely. They color Frederick Douglas as a redhead and Harriet Tubman as a blonde. I could see this happening more easily in a school where the majority of the students are white, but in our classroom, fourteen of the students are not! I think they are not used to learning about African Americans at this school.

Professional Growth Papers

At the end of the each professional semester, I ask preservice teachers to write a professional growth paper, which they present to me in an exit conference. They comment on their participation and effort, the personal goals they have met, and future goals that address additional areas for professional growth. They also write about their teaching insights and present evidence of reflective thinking about their education-related life history in relation to who they are currently as a teacher. As Nicole explained in her professional growth paper:

> I find that I was most comfortable as a student when my emotional needs were met in the class and when I was challenged by varied teaching styles. I know that when I teach, I will work to ensure that my students are comfortable emotionally and are being challenged with a variety of learning experiences. I also recognize that my personal style is different from that of many of the students I encounter. My practicum work has made me especially aware that I must be cautious of generalizing about children. I grew up in an affluent suburban school system. I have learned that regardless of where I teach, I must maintain high standards, but I also must be adaptable and knowledgeable about my environment.

Critical Episodes in Learning

In the second professional semester, preservice teachers complete quick-writes about critical episodes and/or people they can recall from their schooling in social studies and science classrooms. As we look for patterns across their experiences, we usually surmise that what they recall and enjoyed the most were those times when they learned by doing—their enactive experiences—that had relevance, purpose, and meaning in their own lives. They easily claim field trips, science experiments, and drama projects as their most memorable experiences. I use this exercise to come to know of their past schooling, to pull them back to what they enjoyed as children, and to demonstrate that they remember best what they experienced and created. Later, as they plan their lessons, I prompt them to recall their own learning experiences.

In turn, I encourage them to use their students' experiences and backgrounds as springboards for further learning. I also ask them to carefully examine the curriculum packages and activities in teacher resource books. Then I ask them to consider recreating those activities as artists with more concrete activities that are related to the worlds of their students. As a class, we visit our computer laboratory and look at ready-made lessons available on the Internet. Then I try to explain to them that there is a genuine beauty in making their own lessons, especially the ones that don't turn out the way they planned. I ask them to consider how the personal enters their teaching and in what way their lessons relate to the everyday lives of their students.

I share the time I visited my son Lucas, who is a Peace Corps volunteer in Totonicapan, Guatemala. He took me down a long dirt road, through a backyard, and into a local artist's workshop. There I found hand-crafted bowls, crucifixes, and boxes of all sizes. I saw shelves of the artist's finished and unfinished crafts. I smelled the fresh wood and spilled paint. Some of his wares had obvious mistakes and others still needed to be painted, but each was unique and had his imprint and style. I picked up one of the bowls and felt its texture and design. I could feel the artist's intensity and sensed the flow of his experience in making it. The bowl felt different than factory-made ware. I saw the artist smile as I held his work in my hands. I strive to help my students feel ownership in the crafting of their lessons. I sense their creations will be critical learning episodes in their teacher preparation.

Exit Conferences and Interviews

At the end of each semester, I hold individual exit conferences to see what students have learned and what I need to improve upon. My students tell me that I give them more opportunities to design their own lessons than they think they need. I practice my own self-study to see what my students are learning and to have a chance to hear about the mistakes I have made. At the end of each year, we meet again for our second exit conference to review their progress and set new goals for the next semester. I marvel as I watch them develop as teachers. Connie explains:

I need confidence in my own management and handling of situations. Mrs. T. [her cooperating teacher] taught me that if I feel it's right, then it is right as long as I can answer to myself why. I changed so much with regard to just letting things happen and not being so controlling. One thing that has remained the same was my high expectations of the children. I think I've grown because I was so able to try out new things in the classroom.

During exit conferences, I have the opportunity to listen to my students' dilemmas about teaching: being a teacher and/or friend, how to create democratic and motivating classrooms, and how they want to make sure their students can pass standardized tests. I watched how they resolved their dilemmas. During an interview, I asked Alan if he and his partner experimented with a cooperative learning approach in their practicum classroom. I had visited the class and knew that group work was not a common practice used by their cooperating teacher. He replied:

Yes, we did. No matter how often we left the classroom disgusted with our efforts, we never truly lost faith in or respect for our students. We kept coming back and trying to find ways. We asked ourselves, "Where are the good things? Where's the diamond in the rough?" They met our challenges in some cases.

Preservice teachers continue to excite my thinking about teaching, too. I have learned that the times I put the most effort into knowing my students were always the times when I felt I was most successful in teaching them. Nurture matters in teaching and learning, and it includes considering the contexts and cultures that have shaped students' development and their perspectives. Perhaps they will practice that with their own students. Katie and Maryann designed a "Getting to Know You" form for their students so they could incorporate their students' interests in their lessons. In their unit on Washington, D.C., they asked students about their favorite places in Washington and what they knew about the city. They also asked them to describe something unique about themselves or their family. I try to follow my students' work when they student-teach by reading the transformative change section in their action research papers. Diane wrote:

One of the most important lessons that I have learned is that it is imperative for the teacher to understand the culture from which her students come. This was one of my biggest obstacles. I am a Caucasian woman who grew up in a predominantly Caucasian middle-class society, and most of my classroom experiences had been in a similar setting…At various times throughout the semester, I became extremely frustrated with the children as well as myself. Sometimes I even lost my temper. Nevertheless, as I began to understand the needs of the students as well as learn to pace my lessons better, I began to feel successful as a teacher. The nurturing environment fosters learning and builds the self-concepts of the children. I felt that through the autobiography project, I was able to do that to a certain extent. The children were able to learn about each other through sharing their writing with each other. I also tried to use Author's Chair as a means of teaching the children how to say positive things about each other. However, I found that the children did not need to learn how to give compliments. They only needed to be given the opportunity.

In terms of my reflection as a teacher educator, I consider the context, the content, and the learner as I contemplate the many dilemmas embedded in teacher preparation. On a technical level of reflection, educated-related life histories, diverse contexts for viewing self in relation to others, professional growth papers, critical episodes in learning, and exit conferences and interviews are ways I use to know my students' cultural identities as I view them as learners, not clients. On an interpretive level of reflection, the assignments enable me to consider how the socialization of family and community influence our work as students and teachers. On a critical level of reflection, I value knowing preservice teachers' cultures and influences on their development as teachers and believe this knowledge is an essential beginning point in teaching them (see Figure 2.2). Equally important is teaching the content they will need, enhanced through their situated learning, which I present in the next chapter.

❖ Chapter 4
Situating Learning

Vygotskian Principle 2.
Learning occurs during situated and joint activity.

Logbook, 20 August 1999

I was searching for a video at the public library when my eyes came across a video titled "How to Learn to Swim." I couldn't imagine how one could learn to swim out of water and without feedback (unless a VCR was set up right next to a pool as one worked through the motions, which wouldn't be too wise!). We should not be misled into thinking that the Vygotskian concepts of situated learning apply only to people learning to swim. Doesn't that same concept apply to preservice teachers learning to teach?

That it is important to learn something in its context may sound so obvious. Yet many schools of education still prepare preservice teachers superficially, out of the context and dynamics of a classroom or in field experiences that are misaligned to coursework. When they student-teach they often sink rather than swim. In the immediacy of teaching, the learner's lack of experiences can be disastrous. This is why education courses are often criticized for being "too theoretical" and "not very practical." Those that can swim may grow tired, get pulled under by numerous undertows, and eventually drown as they swim alone. I worry about the lack of support systems for teachers. It makes me wonder about the current national shortfall of teachers and the serious attrition rate among teachers.

In his paper on "Psychology and the Teacher" ([1926] 1997), Vygotsky writes:

Ultimately, only life educates, and the deeper that life, the real world, burrows into the school, the more dynamic and the more robust will be the educational process. That the school has been locked away and walled in as if by a tall fence from life itself has been its greatest failing...The teacher's educational work, therefore, must inevitably be connected with his creative, social, and life work (345).

My teaching of preservice teachers is based on the principle that people learn with others in a situated context. Lave and Wenger (1991) claim that learning, thinking, and knowing take place when people are engaged in communal activities, when they situate themselves in a community of practice in the historical development of the activity. Preservice teachers will attest that they learn best in actual classrooms as they listen to cooperating teachers' explicit and implicit instruction and pick up clues from students' interactions as they work within a social, historical, and cultural institution called school. In situated learning, a novice must negotiate and renegotiate entrance into the community, but he or she does so from a peripheral stance, as does the preservice teacher, since the main activity of the classroom teacher is to teach children, not the preservice teacher. Preservice teachers and cooperating teachers do not always share the same perception or definition of the tasks at hand. With peers and cooperating teachers, preservice teachers discuss their education courses and personal theories while they sort out what teaching means. Language plays a key role in mediating the connections, interpretations, and justifications about what they learned and experienced. The context allows preservice teachers to integrate their theories with practice.

Vygotsky ([1960] 1981) believed that cognitive strategies are learned most effectively *during* problem-solving and joint activity. Certain maternal behaviors in mother-child dyads have been found to facilitate the degree to which their babies participate in games, develop language, and learn the rules of a game as the babies become socialized into society (Hodapp, Goldfield, and Boyatzis 1984; Ratner and Bruner 1978; Rogoff, Malkin, and Gilbride 1984). These studies of mother-child interaction are rich with descriptions of how children develop command of a task when the learning is facilitated by the mother's use of repetition, modeling mature performance, dividing the task into components, verbalizing the components of the task, and reinforcing and extending the child's attempts to complete the task (Hodapp, Goldfield, and Boyatzis 1984; Ratner and Bruner 1978; Rogoff, Malkin, and Gilbride 1984). Lave (1977) examined the context and the apprenticeship of new tailors in Liberia, West Africa. She argues that having access to ongoing work and participation in that work were essential components of the learning process of the apprentices, more so than didactic structuring of the task and external evaluations. Greenfield (1984) studied how Zinacanteco children learn to weave with their mothers, and Rogoff (1986) researched how Mayan mothers guide their daughters in learning to weave. In these studies, graduated adaptive interventions were employed to ensure the learner's success and to gradually enable the learner to perform independently. The learners in this study self-regulated; they participated at increasing levels and took greater responsibility for components of the relevant task. These observations were made in real-life situations, not in laboratory settings.

When the teacher mediates while the learner is struggling to figure out how to do the task, he or she may uncover and redirect the learner's misunderstandings of the task, and the learner can then revisit inadequate strategies and reformulate new skills while the teacher is there to guide her/him through it. Internalization develops when the learner is able to integrate skills and practical problem-solving activity with the guidance of a more capable other (Rogoff 1982, 1987; Rogoff and Gardner 1984). Accordingly, skills must be acquired within the context of a specific activity and mediated by a social agent for transfer and decontextualization to occur (Hartup 1985). I was able to study this phenomenon with young children who were learning to solve a puzzle in a computer context with teacher mediation (Samaras 1991). During the interaction, the instructor adopted a tutorial role, intervening and supporting the learners at crucial moments as the learners attempted to solve a problem.

Self-Study Reflection

My big brother John still tells stories about teaching me to balance food while serving at the restaurant. He often helped me clean up the trays of food I spilled. The crashed, turned-over plates with smashed food underneath made my eyes fill with tears. They were symbols of my persistent method of serving by trial and error without a strategy. In contrast, Miss Margie and Miss Bessie didn't rush around, but they were always able to serve their customers with more ease than the fast waitresses like me. I wondered how they did that. I was often paired with Miss Candy for the lunch shift. She showed me how to set up for lunch as she recounted all the housework she had finished before she came to work. I learned from Miss Shirley how to stack trays of filled water glasses to a level that I could carry them without spilling them. With Miss Patti and Miss Linda in my waitress shift team, I learn to fold boxloads of napkins in the shape of royal crowns, and Miss Joan taught me how to tuck napkins securely in breadbaskets to keep the bread fresh for lunch hour. I learned what being prepared for 30 to 40 customers meant. I learned how to use the dysfunctional, yet still somewhat usable, dumbwaiter when I managed special parties in the balcony loft. If you couldn't use the dumbwaiter, you had to climb twenty-five steps with heavy dishes. Balancing heavy dishes lined up and down both of my skinny, bony arms; securing three glasses at a time in my small, cupped hands with the same long fingers that loved to play the piano—all involved a strategy that I learned from more capable others. Maneuvering through a crowd with agility; responding to many requests in a short period of time; filling, without spilling, the sugar and salt and pepper shakers—each became part of my repertoire because of the initiation I received into the restaurant community. My interactions and relationships with my mentors grew stronger over time as I became a permanent member of a very stable restaurant staff. I appreciated those anchors and what I learned from them more over time.

Early in my career I acknowledged that learning needs a situated context and is worthless without a place to see its effects in practice. My brothers and husband studied business and marketing principles in college, but they had no practice. My father understood business models with no formal education in the field because he lived them. He would curse them out for their failing theories and faulty advice even though he made plenty of his own mistakes in his trial-and-error practice. I believe there is a need for a strong theoretical base, but there must be a place to test it in action. It is not that it is only practice that matters, but that the theory is useless without it and vice versa.

Under the tutelage of Carol Seefeldt, a professor in my graduate studies in human development, I developed a guide for creative field trips for young children in which learning was situated in everyday tasks—construction, print-making, making cakes, planting trees. It was sparked by my sons' why questions. In the introduction to the 1980 booklet, I wrote:

> It all started when I was driving down West Street past the new office building under construction and my three-year-old son said, "Stop Mommy. I want to see how the crane works." That gave me the idea and recognition for a book of creative, but seemingly ordinary, things to do with young children in Annapolis. It is filled with the excitement that many adults lose. Through the pristine eyes of my two young sons, with stroller and juice bottle in hand, we traveled downtown to watch potters and sail-makers. Then we went uptown to learn about car repairs and cake designers. We visited the warehouse district of bricks, plumbing sup-

plies, and wood and went out of town on trips to tree and turkey farms and much more. It was all because they reminded me that children just want to know why.

What happens when children go to school? Do students stop caring because learning doesn't make sense out of context? Caine and Caine (1994) remind us that the search for meaning and understanding about the world is oriented toward survival and is basic to the human brain. Situating learning helps students map and see patterns in large amounts of information about the world that they are trying desperately to synthesize and want to learn about.

What happens when preservice teachers go to school? A male speaks of his father's experience in Vietnam. His father explained to him that actually being there and feeling the mud and the heat and listening to farmers' concerns about adequate planting ground (rather than debates about the merits of communism or capitalism) was much different than what someone reads about in a history book. For the most part, new teachers also enter a strange territory with unfamiliar trenches that they have only read about in methods courses. How can preservice teachers practice and situate learning theory? It is commonly recognized that theory needs practice. Practice needs theory, too. Theorists can't know if theory works without its implementation, and practitioners need to know the reasoning and thinking about their practice.

I like what Linda Brodkey (1996) has to say about theory and practice. "Theory can generate a syllabus, but theory only imagines what can happen rather than what does happen to students and teachers. It is research that links theory and practice, for it interrupts the excesses of theorists and practitioners alike by asking the hard questions that might be called the cui bono questions" (244). Theory, no matter how inspiring, has no soul unless the researcher is immersed in the culture and context of doing or practicing it. Nonetheless, it is theory that gives the researcher a frame to examine reality. Dewey (1938) told us a long time ago that knowledge originates in our experiences.

Elbaz (1981) explains that simply because a teacher has a theoretical orientation does not necessarily mean that that theory is the one that teacher uses. Similarly, requiring teachers to claim a philosophy of education for the purpose of having one, or for the career portfolio, does not mean that that is what they use in practice. Nonetheless, the articulation of theory is important to self and others, especially to parents. I believe that regardless of which theory a teacher espouses, he or she needs opportunities to sketch their conceptual and theoretical teaching base with the understanding that it may evolve and shift over time. At points along their professional career, teachers should question if the theory is still believable and valid by situating it in practice.

Throughout my career, I have been determined to link my teaching to research by bringing abstract theoretical knowledge into real settings. Toward that end, a sociocultural model for teacher preparation emerged. In my effort to prepare a more whole teacher, I haven't sheltered preservice teachers from the realities of schools or left them to figure it out by themselves. However, at times my roles as administrator and researcher have distanced me from the realities of school and from the difference between theory and practice. One of my more recent goals was to work with young children again to check the realities of what I teach and how I use my theory in practice.

In the summer of 1999, I was invited to share my interdisciplinary work in curriculum and instruction with children, primarily orphans, and their caregivers who were emotionally traumatized from their experiences in the war-torn Balkan countries. I traveled and worked in partnership with the dynamic Friendship Team Camp Program to Croatia, a largely Catholic country where Serbians are a minority. One of the purposes of the Friendship Team Camp is to teach conflict resolution and cooperation. I helped design and coordinate activities that provided opportunities for children to take the perspectives of others in drama activities. We worked as a team to help promote peace and instill a sense of community among children of various ethnic and religious backgrounds.

With a team of fourteen individuals, I helped to plan and implement the children's camp held at the Peace Center in Selce, Croatia. We also visited a children's home in Rijeka, Croatia, where we met with the director and teachers of the home to research the background and educational needs of the children. This home serves children 3 to 18 years old who for a variety of reasons have no stable place to live. Below is a log of my work:

Logbook, 2 July 1999

People in this charming seaside town called Rijeka don't like to call the children's home an orphanage because these children have parents. But for various reasons, usually poverty or illness, the parents are unable to care for their children. On the day our group is holding a camp for the children, we get lost. When we arrive ninety minutes late, the children are already at the beach for their recess.

We walk down to the seaside, and I gravitate toward a group of young children 3 to 5 years old. I want to test my skills at communicating non-verbally through movement and drama activities, as the other teachers have limited English. One very easygoing and social child approaches me. I start a simple clapping and movement activity with a mirroring of motions that involves a slight but important connection through touch. Soon other children join in. I gradually add a sequence of clapping and assure a redundancy and repetition to the exercise so others who join in can easily learn it. Soon there are eight children and we form a circle. Children move in and out of the activity while we add sound to our movements. When one child decides to sit in the center of the circle, we take turns kneeling and hugging the child, closing in and whispering nonsense sounds. We speak easily through the movement. I hug my colleague Mary in my joy of working with young children again. I will do this again. I must do this again.

Another camp was held at Fuzine, Croatia, at a government-run refugee center of mainly Bosnian children and elders. Daily meetings and prayer were held with the Friendship Team to evaluate and reflect on the work we accomplished. There were other camps planned in Bosnia; however, the Friendship Team church leaders made the decision not to travel to the Bosnian camps due to warnings by the Department of State and the CIA. During the time originally planned for Bosnia camps, I helped construct the Hope Center; I caulked bathrooms, hung curtains, helped prepare dinner. The center used to be an orphanage; now it is used as an international Christian retreat center where youth leaders from around the world develop worldwide efforts toward reconciliation and peace. At each camp, I worked with adults to share *Drama Works*, a handbook developed in an interdisciplinary course that I share with you later in Chapter 8.

Special arrangements were made for me to attend a Serbian Eastern Orthodox church service in Rejika, Croatia, where I was able to meet with a priest and his family. This visit was important in light of the necessity of outreach to bring about reconciliation and reduce the tensions between the members of the cultures of the city. In this service experience, where I was an ethnic minority as an Eastern Orthodox, I found myself asking, "How did I end up here?" and answered it by embracing our human uniqueness and commonality; we are all humans in our one human family. Drama was the conduit.

Ways of Situating Learning

Let's consider the implications of the Vygotskian principle of situating learning for how teachers might be prepared. The premise of my teaching is that, as in natural settings where people learn in families, communities, and the workplace, learning takes place through joint and productive activity; that is, in authentic contexts such as elementary schools and in the context of mutual and shared tasks. It's like my students tell me, "You don't really know about teaching until you're in the situation." Another notes, "Now I understand why I am doing these things and why they work. It gives meaning to what I am doing, and if something that I do does not go as anticipated, I can better analyze the situation, knowing the reason as to why I thought it would work."

To illustrate, I restructured early fieldwork experiences with a reading professor by integrating our coursework in an interdisciplinary unit project with pairs of preservice teachers who were co-teaching under the tutelage of a cooperating teacher. Field experiences include support systems and opportunities for talking aloud about their reflections with cooperating teachers and peers as problems arise. Ideally, coursework should be introduced with field experiences so that students can make immediate and concurrent connections and/or disconnections between the course and fieldwork; for example, readings should be situated in field experiences. In the first professional semester, preservice teachers complete contextualized assignments such as brief papers on topics they have read about and identified in their practicum and a symposium about the School Ethos Project. In the second professional semester, an interdisciplinary unit project with concept maps situates their learning.

Reading-Field Briefs

I assign six reading-field briefs throughout the semester, which are due in written format and then discussed in class. Preservice teachers initially try to summarize portions of an assigned text chapter, which I return to them for a rewrite. The following is an example of one reading-field brief assignment:

> It is imperative that you read about teaching so you can begin to make connections between what you read and what you observe in practice. You can't reflect without experience and observation. Describe your observations from the field

that relate to and validate what you have come to know and understand from this reading. Give examples!

The Teacher
- What do teachers do other than teach? Generate a list after shadowing your cooperating teacher.
- What is an "effective" teacher?
- What do you see as the dimensions of teaching?
- What are some of the decisions teachers have to make?
- Who controls learning in this classroom?
- Does the teacher's conduct reflect the school philosophy? Explain.
- Does the teacher's conduct reflect your teaching philosophy? Explain.
- How much flexibility do teachers have in their planning and implementing of the school's curriculum? How are teachers held accountable for implementing curriculum?

The School Ethos Project

I have also worked to familiarize preservice teachers with the different school cultures that situate their learning in their practicum schools through the School Ethos Project. I ask cohorts to examine their practicum school as if they were anthropologists; they conduct observations, collect data and artifacts, and they interview students, teachers, administrators, and parents to see if what they talk about is what they find in practice as they examine the authenticity of the mission of their practicum school. They investigate the cultural, historical, and philosophical influences on education in the school community. I explain that this is not to be a series of presentations and individual reports. It is group-constructed knowledge in which each person carries individual responsibility for the construction of knowledge and has the experience of working in what Wasser and Bresler (1996) call the "interpretive zone." This joint inquiry is the first dynamically collective assignment I assign where they must collate and interpret field data, hear each other's observations and perspectives, decipher areas of overlap, negotiate, and make meaning of what schooling means at their site.

After researching and synthesizing, they present their School Ethos Project in symposium fashion and learn about the variability of school missions and their authenticity in practice. Below is the actual assignment:

You will be working with other students in your practicum school to develop a presentation of your analysis of your practicum school's ethos. This involves many facets and requires each team member's effort to investigate, ask questions, observe, read, and connect text and class knowledge to the field. Read, research, and collaborate. Take notes. Meet as a group frequently to discuss and synthesize your notes.

Use the following headings for your research and presentation:
- Describe the type of community in which the school is located. Does the school also draw its students from other surrounding communities?
- Describe the school population in terms of socioeconomic and ethnic groups. From what type of homes and backgrounds do students come (e.g., single-parent, recent immigrants)?
- Does the school have an explicit mission and philosophy?
- Does the philosophy take a certain position on any of the dilemmas of schooling (e.g., control, curriculum, or social?) What seem to be the important things stressed at this school?
- Is there authenticity in the mission statement to the enacted curriculum? Describe instances where you saw the school's mission carried out and where it was not. What does the ethos and curriculum of your school mean for teacher planning, teaching for understanding, learning activities, classroom management, and the level of student self-regulation?
- How do the ethos and curriculum connect to child development and learning theories you have learned about from previous education courses? Is there a shared culture or are there shared values at this school? Describe them. What is most valued here? What does this community believe is important about schooling? Does the school represent the culture of the community it serves? Explain. Are there any special ceremonies, traditions, and rituals centered on daily, monthly, and yearly activities? What do these activities mean here?
- What types of family involvement take place at the school? How do the teacher and the school invite families into the classroom? How is the school mission communicated to families?
- Are all families represented at school meetings and events? What input do parents have in decision-making?
- Where is authority located at this school (e.g., administration, teachers, students, families, all)? What are the school rules? Do they reflect the school philosophy? How? How are they known? Who is involved in decision-making? Who has input on the rules? What is the importance of the principal, teachers, students, and families at this school? Is the atmosphere orderly, oppressive, open, etc.? Are there agreed-upon ways of doing things (e.g., collaborating, meeting instructional goals, discipline)? How is discipline handled here? What are considered to be serious problems and how are they handled?
- Examine your school for evidence of the attributes of effective schools as described in your text.
- Describe the school's resources, including technology.

- What aspects of the ethos are most meaningful to you? What causes a problem for you? What ideas would you have for revisions of the school vision? What is the source of those ideas?
- Would you like to teach at this school? Explain.
- Other

Grading Criteria for Symposium on School Ethos (90 pts.)
Research Components: (50 pts.)
1.   depth and quality of individual search (20 pts.)
2.   group's ability to capture and synthesize school ethos of practicum school, depth of search by group (20 pts.)
3.   connections made to learning theories from previous coursework (5 pts.)
4.   data of attributes related to effective schools research (5 pts.)

Presentation Components: (40 pts.)
1.   individual presentation and contribution to group, includes a self-evaluation and team evaluation (10 pts.)
2.   ability to listen when others are speaking and work collaboratively (5 pts.)
3.   substance, quality, creativity, and synergy of group presentation (10 pts.)
4.   handouts/visuals that enhance presentation (15 pts.)

Juliet, who examined the authenticity of the school's philosophy in fostering a diverse student population at an exclusive private school, wrote:

This is an interesting issue and one that I have thought about a lot during the course of my practicum placement. The demographics of my classroom certainly point toward diversity. But if all of the students have advantaged backgrounds and have been assimilated into the dominant culture, is this school really representing diversity in their population?

The Interdisciplinary Unit

Logbook, 27 February 1997

After driving for some time, we came across groups of people gathered along a roadside and stopped to see if they had found a lookout point for the Grand Canyon. We walked anxiously toward the rest stop and gasped. There it was in panorama. I saw the sun shining across a massive transformation of earth and colors splashing before me, and I felt a rush and an emotion that allowed me to embrace for a magnificent and unforgettable moment the natural and authentic connections between science, mathematics, social studies, the arts, and much more. What forces larger than us were at work in this wonder of the world! There was the difference in the scale of the land mass, the reality of water making changes in the earth over time, great depth and breath of land measurement. This was a place where Native Americans had lived, prayed, and died. Snapshots of classic photographs and paintings and the words of poets and of writers flashed through my mind.

Separately, the subjects were like pieces of a jigsaw puzzle begging to be integrated for a coherent wholeness. The integrated scene gave meaning to each piece. I thought, "If the walls of the Grand Canyon could speak, they would tell us of the geologists, the mathematicians, the teachers, the painters, and the poets that each came to the canyon for different reasons and yet for the same reason—to be inspired about their own discipline in the presence of the wholeness and integration of many disciplines.

The assignment that I have found to best situate preservice teachers' learning about teaching is an interdisciplinary unit in an actual classroom. An interdisciplinary teaching model encourages the use of higher-level thinking skills and cooperative skills; at the same time, students acquire content knowledge. Integration of the curriculum is an excellent way to enable preservice teachers to embrace the bigger picture of learning, to perceive and generate patterns, to draw relationships between the past, our society and the world, and our own experiences. Dewey ([1900] 1990) talked about interdisciplinary teaching 100 years ago:

> All studies arise from aspects of the one earth and the one life lived upon it. We do not have a series of stratified earths, one of which is mathematical, another physical, another historical, and so on. We should not be able to live very long in any one taken by itself. We live in a world where all sides are bound together. All studies grow out of relations in the one great common world...The teacher will no longer have to resort to all sorts of devices to weave a little arithmetic into the history lesson, and the like (91).

Preservice teachers work in pairs throughout the spring semester to plan, implement, and evaluate an interdisciplinary unit in their practicum classroom with the guidance of a cooperating teacher. I discussed the interdisciplinary unit assignment in Chapter 2 but focus here on its situated components. They plan and enact science investigation lessons, conduct field trips, integrate technology and family involvement activities in lessons, arrange for resource people to visit classes, work with school specialists, and plan how to individualize learning.

Multisensory and multimedia experiences can enhance visual learning; for example, through seeing paintings or videos, through listening to music, through physical touch or movement, and through the outdoors. Beverly, a preservice teacher who was working with students who have profound and multiple disabilities, found that her students acquired learning in many different ways and with an inner language. She noted the positive cognitive impact of using the outdoors to situate her teaching about the senses and weather. She wrote:

> The students constantly gazed at the snow and rain as it fell upon their delicate faces and hands. They attempted to catch snowflakes with their opened mouths, hoping to identify the taste of snowflakes. One student stated that snow was delicate and delicious. Another student, who was slightly visually impaired, strove to identify what snow felt and looked like using her tactile sense.

The unit project is a microcosm of teaching that enables preservice teachers to begin to see the many facets of their profession. Although the unit is housed within my social studies and science methods course and centers on a social studies or science theme (e.g., rainforests, communities, weather), professors from the reading, mathematics, and health and physical education methods courses also have interdisciplinary assignments in the unit and the field experience.

Depending on who is teaching the other methods courses, some cohorts have experienced more integration in methods courses than others. I have also been working on more collaboration with other arts and sciences faculty who teach subject courses that preservice teachers take in order to meet licensure and university distribution requirements. These other courses comprise two-thirds of their program of studies but are not necessarily aligned to what they will need to know as teachers in elementary schools. For example, the music department offers a course in teaching music in the elementary school and the science department has offered environmental education courses. This is an area I need to work on more; I sense it slipping away as faculty position themselves to do more solo work.

In their final exit conference papers, preservice teachers commented that professors were willing to offer lesson ideas and critiques throughout the semester, but for some, that was not enough. A comment by Monica in an exit conference tells me there is a need for greater cooperation among education professors, which is where I began this whole project. Her comments remind me that restructuring is a continuous process:

The fieldwork and coursework support one another. I can see how the things we are learning in class work for us within the classroom. I wish that all of the assignments were tailored toward the unit. I felt we could have focused on the whole-language assignments. I was really disappointed I couldn't implement something from classroom management because that was one of our major concerns with our class.

There are many other teaching tasks, on both a smaller and a larger level, that are part of the repertoire of a preservice teacher; for example, developing a science learning center or placing their unit within a year-long curriculum. The unit requires them to continuously communicate with each other, with professors, and with their cooperating teacher and to think about what they are learning in their course and what they are experiencing in the field. It gives preservice teachers an opportunity to test their practical theories and knowledge bases in a real setting while also learning about pre-active, interactive, and post-active planning. In Richard's interview, he explained:

We've learned that we've had to take the situation we were placed in and alter what we would get in class to that situation, and it worked. In some cases, it didn't [work], but we would always talk about it. We were constantly going over it with our teachers, and we got a lot of feedback from the principal. We're in it and we see the situation.

Cooperating teachers, and sometimes principals, observe preservice teachers while they are teaching and offer their comments. Students are videotaped as they teach; their peers view the videotape and comment on their teaching. The students also complete a self-evaluation of their videotaped teaching. When they see themselves, it seems easier for them to change because they can see their strengths and mistakes and talk about them with others. They can also see classroom events they have read about. A preservice teacher remarked that the distance the videotape of her teaching provided allowed her to look at the class objectively and see what was going on. It helped sanction constructive criticism from a peer because of the equal footing or, as one claimed, "being able to see a peer who was going through many of the same dilemmas that I found in teaching." Better yet, they listen to the observations of their peers, as Gloria wrote to her partner in a peer review:

I saw that you lost your composure at one point when the children would not stop talking and listen to you. That was an extremely touchy situation. The bell you rang did not work. Try lowering your voice.

They finally see if, and how, their teaching makes a difference in children's learning, although they rarely admit any connections of coursework to practice. It is my belief that the reason many teachers perceive the student-teaching experience as the most useful part of their teaching preparation (Feiman-Nemser and Buchmann 1985) is because they are able to experience and make sense of what they read about in methods courses. It is not that more time in the field experience matters as much as what occurs in the field. Preservice teachers need opportunities to not only observe but to experience what they are learning about in methods courses. They typically don't do that in any concentrated manner until student teaching. Cynde excitedly reported:

> I loved the fact that you offer course fieldwork before student teaching. I think that was the greatest thing I learned. You learn from the books, but it all comes together when you're in the classroom.

For some, the connections are more subtle and latent. Stephy stated:

> Almost unknowingly, I took everything from the classroom that I had learned from the book and then actually did it...So later I realized, "Oh, this is what they were talking about when we learned these different strategies."

In the unit, preservice teachers revisit their earlier education courses and situate prior knowledge. For instance, they demonstrate knowledge from their psychology of education course in the pre-planning section of their unit by discussing the theoretical assumptions that inform their teaching and the planned unit activities. The activities in their lessons include what they have come to understand about motivation and linking prior knowledge. Preservice teachers also discuss human development issues in their unit such as the developmental appropriateness of their theme to the children they are teaching, the rationale of its content and the presentation they chose, individualized assessment to maximize all children's learning, and motivational issues.

They are asked to note the current assumptions they hold about the teaching and learning process, which are embedded in their own education-related histories and their teaching experiences. The school ethos project, conducted in the first professional semester, prepares them for an analysis and description of their particular classroom setting, the classroom management system, and the school's learning atmosphere. In some situations, it will remind them of the limitations on the changes they can institute in classrooms while they are teaching in a practicum.

Not surprisingly, a preservice teacher comments, "I talked to other teachers and actual professionals outside of our practicum and they were skeptical about the interdisciplinary units. They just think it's a bunch of pretty little theories and is nothing of value. In some situations, I do think it works. I've looked at the studies, and it can work." It seems unfair to ask preservice teachers to identify with particular theories when they are just learning them. I remind them that I've been at it for almost thirty years, but they must begin to articulate what they believe. Furthermore, when teachers have difficulty explaining their theories, especially to parents, it disempowers them (Samaras 1994b).

Concept Maps

As I noted earlier, I teach about and assess concept attainment through preservice teachers' contextualized and situated experimentation using pre-planning and post-planning concept maps of unit planning. In the beginning of the semester, I ask preservice teachers to draw a pre-planning concept map of their understanding of unit planning (see sample in Figure 4.1).

At the end of the semester, I ask them to draw a post-planning concept map of their notions of unit planning (see sample in Figure 4.2). In this manner, I obtain a visual representation of what they know and what they need to know about long-term planning in the pre-planning concept map, and then what they have learned through their post-planning concept map.

In a similar vein, I ask each preservice teacher to draw a pre-planning concept map of their background knowledge of the content of the unit topic (see sample in Figure 4.3). Then after researching and while teaching, they draw a post-planning concept map of their background knowledge of content (see sample in Figure 4.4). The pairs divide the research content, create, and share their post-planning concept maps. As learners, they discover the gaps in their knowledge about planning and content. They are able to observe the shifts in their own planning and knowledge of content. I am able to see and follow their growing under-standing about planning and the subject matter they are researching. Most important, they begin to understand that they can learn the material they need to teach and should learn it.

During the semester, they write about their background knowledge in a paper that is reshaped by contributions from peers, professors, and the cooperating teacher throughout the semester. Through their situated learning, they recognize that they might need to narrow their scope. They may decide to implement a focused rather than a broad view of their topic. They ascertain what they still need to know based on their students' questions and divide the research. Much to their surprise, they find out that young children ask especially difficult questions, as do older ones. Vickie and Frosina state: "We too were learning about various aspects of the Civil War. We also found that we were often challenged by our students, answering questions, initiating motivation to learn, and developing tasks that would address their individual talents and ability levels." This knowledge construction will enable them to see how lessons can link and build upon other lessons. It also allows them to experience what they want their students to do—to make connections between pieces of information.

Reading-field briefs, the School Ethos Project, and the interdisciplinary unit with concept mapping are just a few of the ways I have used to address the dilemma of how I could situate preservice teachers' learning on a technical level. As I have shared throughout this chapter, an interpretive level of reflection has enabled me to consider what situated learning means to my students. I have solicited their feedback and interpretation of its usage each semester. A critical level of reflection has led me to understand why situated learning is an essential component of teacher preparation (see Figure 2.2).

Looking back to the three major program goals (presented in Chapter 2), the interdisciplinary unit has served as an excellent project in offering the following:

- providing preservice teachers with a coherent experience of developing curriculum in action
- giving preservice teachers opportunities to carry out a sequence of instruction
- giving preservice teachers an opportunity to learn from their cooperating teachers and to try out instructional practices advocated in coursework

The unit situates their coursework in a real classroom with cognitive, collegial, and emotional support. Students work long and hard on the unit and state that they feel a sense of ownership and pride in their work at the end of the semester. As they work in communities of practice with support from peers and cooperating teachers, they slowly begin to recognize that learning to teach doesn't mean figuring out everything by yourself.

I continue to reflect and study ways to improve upon preservice teachers' learning through situated learning. For example, one of the weaknesses of the program I identified through preservice teachers' reflective journals was that they knew little about the culture of school families. There were no field experiences that situated their learning about family involvement. Preservice teachers had almost no contact with parents, and the contact they did have was mainly negative, especially in the less affluent schools. Student teachers criticized how parents would spend money to purchase kindergarten graduation robes but wouldn't send in money for field trips. They were disappointed in parents' lack of school involvement. In 1995, Andrea, a preservice teacher, wrote:

> In all of my schooling experiences, the children had parents who were committed to helping their sons and daughters. They were always willing to volunteer time and be involved. I was shocked when I attended a back-to-school night and saw that only six parents or guardians attended in my classroom of 37 children.

In 1996, I conceived the First Teachers program as a way to address this issue. With my students at my side and along with my dear friend "Jo" Wilson, then the director of field experiences at CUA, we visited a district school surrounded by and drawing almost all of its population from two public-housing complexes. On the playground, we recruited families to First Teachers, a sociocultural-based after-school program to involve families. Preservice teachers came to know the inner-city community through families' computer-documented oral histories. Preservice teachers heard firsthand the difficulties poverty could bring to children's learning.

Family members worked with their children after school in a classroom or media center; they moved through four learning centers to create computer-documented family oral histories. They took turns telling their stories at the Talking Center. Oral tradition through storytelling has been an essential component of teaching about culture, particularly for African-American families. Storytelling can mediate higher levels of thinking, build relationships, and foster a sense of community (McNamee 1990). Stories can also teach the values of belonging, ethnicity, and confirmation of self-worth and can document a history of a family's faith and resilience (Hale 1991). Many children also wanted to draw accompanying pictures of the stories at the Drawing Center. Then they wrote the story out at the Writing Center and typed it at the Computer Center. They wrote of their past, their family identity, their roots, and their culture and created a family album to share together and with others. Families served as cultural mediators who motivated, supported, and sustained the ideas of the children through writing. Education students assisted in facilitating the process, served as computer trouble-shooters as needed, and helped families organize the stories for their final family story album. From a Vygotskian standpoint, First Teachers provided a shared activity, or culturally mediated instruction, to facilitate children's internalization of mental processes and the tools of culture such as language, narrative, problem-solving, and the use of technology.

It all made sense theoretically, but Jo and I faced many problems in launching and maintaining the program, which might or might not have been alleviated with more funding. We stood in overheated school hallways, old schoolyards, and parking lots to distribute flyers to families. In our efforts to promote the program, we gave presentations at back-to-school nights, school meetings, and award assemblies. We insisted on not giving token awards to families, even though most have been conditioned by schools in that manner. Above all, we respected their story contributions as gifts to their children. Once families came, they typically continued to come.

Jo noted that family members were willing to make the sacrifice. They were willing to walk back to school to meet their child for the program, leave work early, or get relatives involved to support students. However, the schools just weren't ready for after-school programs, no matter how appealing it seemed to the students. We had trouble negotiating the use of computers and rooms, and often the computers did not work properly. Sometimes we waited in hallways for classrooms to be unlocked by the custodian. We had hope and the determination to get the programs up and running, which we finally did, although the program did not sustain itself after we left. We did not have the dedicated support of principals and teachers to help recruit or work with families in the program.

There were also scheduling difficulties and competing school agendas, and we lacked significant grant money. First Teachers wasn't received as a departmental adventure but rather as Anastasia and Jo's project. Jo and I were managing the program with the assistance of a handful of student volunteers. Sometimes I taught the extra children that parents brought along to the sessions while Jo helped set up the family member with the child at the computer. A teacher who agreed to let us use her room exclaimed, "That's why I don't do these kinds of programs, because I don't want to have to babysit all the other kids they bring along." She also expressed concern about the young visiting siblings and cousins who were playing with her classroom toys. We tried to recruit more student volunteers. Some of our student teachers at the schools agreed to participate with us, but their attention and time was concentrated on surviving the student-teaching experience. Even when we transported our program to a neighborhood school, there were conflicts with students' course schedules. Jo drove her van by students' classes as they let out so she could quickly get them to the school while I ran to the school to set up the learning centers.

Although we worked very hard, I believe the major difficulty was that the program was not owned enough by school faculty for it to continue. It is imperative to gain full and ongoing school support. No one wanted the extra work of coordinating it if Jo and I weren't there to keep it going. Some teachers who wanted to work with us were compelled to use the after-school time to tutor students for upcoming standardized testing. Teachers were tired by the end of the day or they needed that time to devote to working with students or they left school early because they were completing graduate coursework. What they couldn't see was that their teaching would be easier because of the connections they could make with their students and families in a relaxed atmosphere. I see myself returning to that effort.

While volunteering at the schools, we gained family permission to make copies of their stories and conduct interviews with them. Through the interviews, parents told us that one of the major attractions to the program was that they and their children could learn about using a computer. The computer allowed families to write, save, and print their stories easily. However, it was the human factor of interaction and support and the responsiveness of family members that attracted my attention. I found similar scaffolding structures to the ones I had noted in teacher-child dyads (Samaras 1996). The computer provided a context for cognitive change, one that fostered sociocultural learning opportunities between children and their families. We found that the program provided an avenue for families, regardless of educational level, to mediate family values and culture and to interact with other families in a community where it looked like no one cared (Samaras and Wilson 1999). Greater access to parents and community did begin to broaden preservice teachers' perspectives of families. An education student made note of this:

I had to remind myself not to judge how she [a mother] interacted with her daughter. They obviously had a loving relationship but it was rougher than what I was accustomed to. It was a challenge to remain nonjudgmental about parenting styles.

I did a lot of volunteering at my children's elementary school to resituate my own learning. I observed how little school had changed since I was a student. My hope was renewed when I worked alongside creative teachers and learned from them. Serving as a consultant to federally funded childcare centers also reminded me of the crucial work needed for young children's education and care, as did rich discussions with Pat Kinney, who worked diligently for quality childcare. During my sabbatical, I volunteered at a high school child development laboratory where adolescents who wanted to be teachers taught young children. I worked mainly with African-American females, helping them with lesson planning and their interactions with the children. I tried to demonstrate that lessons weren't just in the lesson activities books that filled their school shelves. There is so much work to do.

My latest endeavor to stay in touch with situating theory and practice connections is a project called The Magic College Bus that I have initiated with Lynn Ringenberg, who is a university-school practicum liaison. We arranged for theory-to-practice visits in schools and piled preservice teachers into Lynn's van to visit schools so they could see and discuss what we were talking about in class. We met with our current students, teachers, and our graduates who are now teaching in neighborhood schools. With our students, we observed their teaching and spoke to them about the realities they found.

On another school visit, we walked through beautifully designed early childhood classrooms, noting the contributions by families and the use of technology. Lynn and I conducted floor training, or speaking about what was occurring, while we observed teaching in action with our students. Later, at a nearby coffeehouse, we extended our discussion about what we thought about the hidden curriculum and the school politics we observed. We all enjoyed our escape from the ivory tower as we used practice for the ultimate testing ground of our theories. I know I must continue to situate learning both for my students and myself.

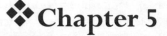

❖ Chapter 5
Structuring Social Mediation

Vygotskian Principle 3.
Cognition is always socially
mediated, especially through language.

Logbook, 13 January 2001

    I attend a voice recital of Peabody Preparatory students with my daughter Athena. As the young vocalists nervously perform, I notice the voice teacher mouthing the words of their opera pieces, raising her eyebrows on the high notes, and moving her hands wildly about in her seat. She understands well what each student must do and has used speech and expression in her social exchanges with them to move them toward that understanding. She looks like she wants to sing for them but knows that she cannot. They must internalize how to sing the Italian love words passionately, how to get the audience to follow their moves and hear their song.

    This scene reminds me how difficult it is to teach. I try to be responsive to my students, to the classroom contexts in which they must work, and to the issues they struggle to understand. I know I can be a support to them, but they have to feel and internalize what teaching is all about. I am only part of the mentoring system that helps them internalize what they learn. Dialogue with my students provides the means to influence their thinking. Maybe teacher educators are sounding boards who only play back the misconceptions of preservice teachers so they might understand them the second or third time they hear them. Maybe teacher educators are deliverers of mythical, mystical messages like those from the Oracle of Delphi that students must then decode. At any rate, watching the voice teacher reminds me that teaching is not telling. Teaching involves mentoring students in their development as they appropriate and create an internal understanding of a task.

According to Vygotsky (1978), cognition is always socially mediated, or influenced by others in social interaction. However, individuals must internalize cognition. Merely mimicking a teacher is not cognition. Thinking begins on the interpersonal, or social, plane before it can be internalized as intrapersonal knowledge. Learning, thinking, and knowing arise through collaboration and reappropriating feedback from others. In contrast to animals, humans have the capacity to explain their understanding of an experience with other members of their social group. It is a profoundly social process that depends on external tools, such as problem-solving techniques, memory strategies, computers, art, and music, especially through internal sign systems such as language and writing. Vygotsky emphasized the role that language plays in instruction as a key factor in mediated cognitive growth.

Vygotsky was interested in the social origins of human development and recognized that physical and cultural growth work in synergy. The learner's developmental capabilities are enhanced through social interaction. He formulated the general laws of cultural development whereby higher mental functions are internalized in a sociocultural system. He states, "Any function in the child's cultural development appears twice, or on two planes. First it appears on the social plane, and then on the psychological plane. First it appears between people as an interpsychological category, and then within the child as an intrapsychological category" (Vygotsky [1960] 1981, 163). Although Vygotsky argued that collective activities promote learning, he stated that cognition is enhanced through a process of internalization in learning dyads.

Two lines of development are described in Vygotsky's work: primitive, natural, or elementary forms and cultural or higher mental functions (Stone 1985; Wertsch 1985). Natural lines of development are elementary functions that are unmediated activities. They arise from children's direct interaction with the environment; that is, elementary forms of perception that do not include operation on non-concrete objects or abstract speech as it relates to the functional significance of actions. Cultural lines use cultural sign systems in order to mediate between elementary functions and higher psychological or mental functions. Included are functions such as voluntary memory, logical memory, selective attention, and especially language as a way that humans represent their understandings of the world. Each of these higher-order functions is abstract and is influenced by social interactions. None of them function fully in the young child.

Vygotsky believed that theory and practice were inexorably connected and mutually dependent. Scientific or formal knowledge originates in everyday knowledge. He emphasized that from birth, children engage in interactions with other children and with adults who socialize them into their culture through their interactions and use of signs or symbolic tools. In the twenty-first century, this is accomplished through socially mediated tools such as hands and computers and through culturally based signs such as language and writing. The role of society is to mediate between mature approaches to cultural inventions and strategic action. Thus, adults guide the skills of each generation, leaving a legacy in the form of technologies such as literacy, number systems, and computers as well as value systems, scripts, and norms for handling new situations (Rogoff 1987).

According to Vygotsky, social regulation also occurs when adults analyze problems for children because the child does not yet have ample cognitive power to do so or a specific representation of how to solve the problem. The learner must be allowed to participate and regulate part of the problem-solving activity but within a level of cognitive understanding in relation to the difficulty of the task. When the learner works in a dialogic setting and his or her partner can help the learner regulate the process (the interpsychological plane), he or she then has the tools to regulate the process independently and internalize it (the intrapsychological plane). Wertsch and Hickman (1987) note that verbal and nonverbal guidance are both crucial ingredients for making the transition from other to self because it allows the learner to construct a representation of the goal and the strategic means to define and accomplish it.

The interchange between a teacher and a learner may be the most effective instructional setting in which to teach learners of any age. Studies suggest that learning interchanges need not be limited to teacher and student and can include peers or those more capable than the student in a specific area (Azmitia 1988; Forman and Cazden 1985; Tudge and Rogoff 1989). For example, in the Forman and Cazden (1985) study, 9-year-olds were given a problem-solving task about chemical reactions. In the initial planning stages of the task, children demonstrated collaborative problem-solving by taking turns in offering their expertise. Later in the task, children solved the same problem independently. Similarly, Doolittle (1995) found that sixth-graders in a computer science class advanced their writing skills when they worked with high school students because of the authentic task and situation, the social interaction, and a metacognitive change.

I have experienced the cognitive and affective power of learning with others in various learning and teaching contexts□when I tutored a child in an urban renewal project for my college sociology class, when I taught my children Greek folk dances, when I learned to tend a garden from my father by working alongside him. I learned a little about farming and a lot about how we learn through others through cooperative ventures.

One of our recent teacher education program projects was to establish a database of our alumni that includes our graduates' teaching employment and/or advanced degrees. As I read through the lists of graduates, I found that most had secured teaching jobs or had graduated from prestigious graduate schools. I felt so proud of them and was overjoyed that they had passed my way. I am reminded of Kahlil Gibran's (1923) assessment of the effective teacher:

> The teacher who walks in the shadow of the temple, among his followers, gives not of his wisdom but rather of his faith and his lovingness. If he is indeed wise he does not bid you enter the house of his wisdom, but rather leads you to the threshold of your own mind (62).

I often reflect on how to lead and guide my students to the thresholds of their minds through my faith in their abilities and with a sense of care as we developed learning relationships. As Bullough and Pinnegar (2001) suggest, I push to improve the learning situation not only for them but for myself as well. Fromm (1956) stated the paradox:

> But in giving, [mankind] cannot help bringing something to life in the other person, and this which is brought to life reflects back to him. In truly giving, he cannot help receiving that which is given back to him...In the act of giving something is born, and both persons involved are grateful for the life that is born for both of them (24–25).

Relating to another person while working toward a common goal was always the most exciting part of learning and teaching to me. During my doctoral work, I wrote on my notions of a 3 R's curriculum—reciprocity, responsiveness, and respect—and how it related to my assumptions about teaching and guidance (Samaras 1989). Reciprocity is the teacher-child interchange, or the give and take during a specific learning activity that allows the teacher to help transform the learner's thinking by modifying the difficulty of tasks and mediating more mature strategies. Responsiveness is an ongoing dance between the teacher and learner where the teacher is sensitive, analytical, and reactive to the learner's engagement and understanding. Respect is the teacher's acknowledgment of each student's social and cultural history and ability to construct new knowledge. Intuitively, I was dabbling in notions of intersubjectivity, or the joint understanding of a topic achieved through dialogue, collaboration, and perspective-taking. What I had arrived at on my own was a proto-Vygotskian model. Vygotsky's sociocultural theory helped me make sense of my ideas about learning through others.

A critical incident in my understanding of social mediation occurred during my graduate assistantship, when I was apprenticing with Sara Smilansky, a visiting professor at the University of Maryland, College Park, who was a clinical psychologist and early childhood specialist from Israel. We team-taught early childhood majors. At the end of each class, Sara would ask our students if they had learned anything from us. At first I thought, "Oh no. What if they say no?" Then I thought, "What if they did? That would be good to know." The collective and public review of our teaching was also a chance for students to make sense of what they thought they learned and co-construct knowledge in a dialogic atmosphere. Sara pushed me as a neophyte professor to ask the really difficult questions although she knew I was worried that others might find out that some students didn't learn from us. I am grateful to Sara because this inquiry of seeking students' perspectives helped lay a foundation for my self-study of teaching practices. And Sara taught me that just as we had a chance to correct our teaching after feedback from our students, the students benefited from a chance to resubmit their work for our class. They plowed what they learned back into their resubmitted work; typically, the reworked material was their best work.

As I think back to one of the most difficult years of my life, I vividly recall my first year of teaching. I wish I could have had more experience as an intern with a supportive school-university context and with mentors to mediate my learning. Complicating my inexperience as a teacher, I received no field experiences until student teaching. Aligning field experiences with early coursework would later become one of my major goals as a teacher educator. As a rookie teacher, I found myself with no induction system or structure for social mediation. I was willing to be individually responsible for my teaching, but there was no professional team, mentor, or collaboration with the mutual goal of improving overall school instruction. As with many novice teachers, I was given several courses and ability levels to teach, which meant multiple class preparations. I had the students who needed the most help and I was also assigned as an advisor to extracurricular activities such as serving as the teacher representative of the Citizen's Advisory Board, coaching the volleyball team, and coordinating the drill team.

Several teachers guarded their boring ditto-master books and hoarded the best resources. That is not to say there were not other teachers who were sensitive to my situation, but they had to get through their own days. Maybe they thought that an offer of help would make me feel inadequate. After all, only students are supposed to ask for help. Besides, the system was not set up for collegiality and offered no incentives for mentoring or team-teaching.

I wanted to hold class discussions and I did, although with great difficulty and not always successfully. This seemingly simple strategy that I learned in my social studies methods course would prove very challenging in a school where "lower-track" students were not given opportunities to develop skills in the art of dialogue. Many veteran teachers warned me about being too soft or trying those fancy useless things I learned at the university. I'll never forget when one student looked at me with anguish and said, "Please just give us the dittos like everyone else does. What are you trying to do to us?" What was I trying to do to them? Those early teaching days fluctuated with episodes of failure and success.

Logbook, 16 July 2000

I drive down West Street; the same street where I grew up fifty-one years ago that is one block from where I had my first teaching job thirty years ago. I see Maria, one of my former students, walking. I taught her in my first year of teaching. She was a quiet girl and now I see her as a woman in her bright yellow uniform as she walks to her job at the local grocery store. She is wearing a pair of fanciful sunglasses that stand out against her otherwise simple presentation. I've seen her walking many times before; wearing her yellow uniform and red sunglasses that seem to shout out something about her I do not understand. I feel like I didn't get to know her enough to teach her well. Could I have done more for her as her teacher? I was so desperately just trying to survive as a novice and rookie. I was so on my own in my teaching that year.

In my second year of teaching, I was fortunate to team up with Kathy Lawson, who also taught seventh-grade geography, one of the three teaching preparations I had that year. She had been teaching for a year and knew how to do long-term planning. She taught me about balancing the demands of school and life and became my lifelong friend. We spent long afternoons with coffee and cookies at her nearby apartment as she mediated new notions of planning. Collaboration can make learning easier.

I found collegiality and shared cognition again in my high school teaching. I joined two colleagues as part of a social studies team. We helped open a new school under the principalship of a man we all respected highly. Now, as I look back, I see that I received mediation from colleagues, yet not enough, and not consistently enough. Collaboration and mentoring are essential after teacher preparation, but ideally they should be part of teacher education. When I became a teacher educator, I structured activities that promoted collaboration and collegiality during teacher preparation so that preservice teachers could benefit from these essential ingredients of teacher development.

I later became a part of teaching teams at two universities and was able to extend my knowledge about interdisciplinary learning in language arts and early childhood education, where I team-taught with exceptional professors such as John O'Flahavan, who also practiced Vygotskian theory. Each time, I grew professionally and gained new insights through co-planning, co-teaching, and co-presenting at educational conferences with outstanding individuals (Samaras and Pour 1992, 1993). In the interim, I continued to experiment with strategies that moved away from the more normative didactic styles I had used in my early teaching. I often reminded myself how unappealing they were to me as a student. Class sessions involved research inquiries that students presented in roundtable or symposium formats. In the formative stages of the paper, students received feedback from their peers and professor during class.

I enjoy my teaching immensely. My best and most interesting teaching and research experiences have involved a team effort toward a mutual goal. In my classes, I emphasize that seeking and giving strategic support serves everyone. For example, my interest in the arts led me to seek out an art teacher who mentored me in becoming a "picture person," or an elementary school volunteer who teaches concepts and content through reproductions of fine art. Susan would join me later when I taught preservice teachers (Samaras and Pheiffer 1996).

In 1992, I was a full-time visiting assistant professor of education at CUA. I am most grateful for the beginning support from a few good mentors inside and outside the university. I had many rich intellectual discussions with Nancy Taylor about program development. We met regularly and I listened attentively to her research agenda and strategies.

She taught me about the importance of teaching concepts and about the politics that permeate academe. Linda Valli gently guided me in my transition to director of teacher education. Dave Martin supported my beginning involvement in professional organizations. We had long conversations by phone and by e-mail about orchestrating a symposium on professional development for student teachers in the metropolitan area. Knowing that there were others who could and would mentor me as a novice professor eased my entrance into the academic community.

In 1993, I would be invited to join the department as a tenure-track assistant professor. Again, I had to handle many hats as professor, director of teacher education, chair of the teacher education committee, certification officer, coordinator of national and state accreditation, advising coordinator, coordinator of the undergraduate and graduate elementary programs, and coordinator of the graduate teacher certification program. Like other professors, I taught numerous classes and served on many department and university committees. I also tried to research, write, and be a wife and mother.

Consequently, my oldest son became a gourmet chef for the family. While I was struggling to balance my new professional roles in academe, I had my second back surgery, helped get two children off to college, and dealt with the harsh realities of everyday life. These experiences tested my early training in the restaurant on multiplicity and simultaneity to its limits. My mother, husband, sister Irene, and mother-in-law offered their help, as did childcare sitters and other family members and friends. I don't pretend that I was able to accomplish my work without assistance or that I was a "Super Mom" I will attest that I worked all the time—long, hard, and seemingly forever—with great self-discipline. My mother gave me the inner strength I needed to carry me through the most complicated years. At work I built layers of resiliency and wore my battle scars proudly, especially when I felt like I worked alone.

Logbook, 14 December 1998

I watch a star runner at a track meet today. He runs through the finish line in a team relay, moving his team into first place. Several other runners in his heat run up to him after the race and attempt to embrace him. But the runner looks distant, uncomfortable, and uncertain of their energy and purpose. Perhaps, in his mind, he has learned to run the race alone and for himself. After all, he has been rewarded handsomely for that in the past.

Unfortunately, in academia, too, the system often rewards independent rather than collaborative effort. I was told in the tenure process that it was essential that I have individual articles because it would be difficult for evaluators to know how much I had contributed in co-authored research, even if I was the first author. Joint service efforts especially were not considered to be serious work. So I did both. As I raced around, with the deadline for tenure application approaching, many of my publications were still out for review. In my sixth year at the university, a professor asked me if I wanted to drop my tenure line in exchange for an administrative one to secure my position for the department as director of teacher education because "You're so good at it." I said, "No thanks. I am going for the gold." Like the women who served in World War II, I told myself, "The hell I can't!" (even if it almost killed me). My publications were accepted, even the ones I thought might not be. Several people guided me as I walked over the coals of the tenure process. In 1999, I received promotion and tenure, worn out but victorious and with great support from the dean and the provost. It was a glorious moment; I had tenure and I had remained true to my early convictions about teaching.

Ways of Structuring Social Mediation

Logbook, 3 March 2001

Today I attended an orchestra concert where my daughter played her violin. During intermission, I spoke to a former high school teaching colleague who despises cooperative learning, or at least how he sees educators using it. He said that in an unbalanced heterogeneous classroom, a few students do all the work, the result of which is that each student does not feel equally responsible for the learning process, the cognitive load, or the group effort. He explained that the orchestra is a good example of effective cooperative learning, where each student contributes to the group by practicing individually, in sectionals, and as a total group. They each contribute toward a successful collaborative effort, but it is really more than cooperative learning because the process involves social mediation. During a practice, I watch how the conductor speaks to them and instructs them toward their goal of making music as a community. Who orchestrates beginning teachers' entrance into a school setting? Who mediates them toward a shared accomplishment?

A colleague identified me as a "cooperative learning" researcher because it was a way for him to explain, or at least try to encapsulate, the Vygotskian principles I integrate in my teaching. Other colleagues better understood my work as it relates to intersubjectivity, or arriving at a shared understanding and perspective of a common goal, such as developing an interdisciplinary unit. It is not just "cooperative learning." From a Vygotskian stance, preservice teachers actively construct their understandings through a process of appropriation and through dialogue and interaction with others (Leont'ev 1981).

There is research to support the idea of community-centered environments (Bransford, Brown, and Cocking 1999) and social mediation and cognitive change for children engaged in a social studies unit (Newman, Griffin, and Cole 1989). Just as children do, preservice teachers benefit from talking about what they are learning. They are most interested in listening to the peers who are working on similar teaching tasks and goals (Ball 2000; Wells 2000). I incorporate much classroom dialogue so my students can make meaning of their experiences. I encourage cooperation, negotiation, and problem-solving through peer coaching and paired and cohort structures. Later, I learned that others describe such pedagogical structures as feminist (Erdman 1990; Hulse-bosch and Kocrner 1994).

For preservice teachers, collective cognition can include learning about pedagogical knowledge, knowledge of subject matter content, and knowledge of self and learners. Preservice teachers can develop a deeper understanding of teaching when they are given opportunities to work together in shared tasks and with common goals. And interdisciplinary units frame a need to know through dialogue, negotiation, and production.

The nature of the unit assignments requires students to learn that they must work together, although some have acquired better negotiating and social skills than others. In a way, they seem to work harder because, as one student stated, "I don't want to let my partner down." They enter into a working relationship that typically leads to mutual trust and fine efforts. I have not found one preservice teacher who was less committed than his or her partner. If anything, they each make an effort to highlight their contributions to the cooperating teacher and to me. Their ability to establish a good rapport with their cooperating teacher, accept feedback easily, and learn from others while still keeping their own identity are all essential components of how easily they are able to establish a good fit and be welcomed into the school culture and community of teachers.

Throughout the yearlong education course and fieldwork, I structure opportunities for peer and cooperating teacher interactions that use dialogue as the central medium for teaching, learning, and personal theory-building. Some of the ways I do that is through using the Author's Chair exercise, through pair and cohort mediation, through shadowing, and through poster sessions. I use the Author's Chair assignment in the beginning of the spring semester so I can begin to understand their thinking about planning the unit.

The Author's Chair

Below is the actual assignment:

> You are asked to share the Author's Chair format below and receive feedback on your unit draft with your peers during class and your cooperating teacher at your practicum school. Some of our best ideas generate from working closely with our colleagues. We will explore the use of the Author's Chair as a means for sharing our unit drafts that need feedback, suggestions, development, and elaboration. The term Author's Chair comes from language arts and is an activity where writers present their own writing to peers who may ask questions of the author. The Author's Chair facilitates perspective-taking, celebrates the process of authoring, establishes linkages between writers and readers, and emphasizes the social dimensions of learning.
>
> Author's Name:
> Grade Level of Teaching:
> Cooperating Teacher and School:
> Theme Topic of Interdisciplinary Unit:
> Please be ready to share #1–4 below with your peers in class and submit #1–7.
> 1. Central Question and Rationale: What is it you are trying to do and why?
> 2. Concepts: (single words) Sub-concepts
> 3. Generalizations (preliminary): (use sentences)
> 4. Unit Objectives: cognitive, critical thinking skills, and social skills; values; general knowledge objectives embedded in your unit
> 5. Materials and Resources:
> 6. Your Wonderful Ideas and Activities That Support Your Central Question:
> 7. Means of Evaluation:
> 8. Peer Suggestions:

Below is an example of notes I wrote as I observed students using the Author's Chair format:

Logbook, 8 October 1993

Evan uses the Author's Chair to talk about his initial ideas about a unit he has planned. He shares his thinking about his planning ideas with his peers and professors, who present questions and offer feedback. He will begin implementing his unit on "Mapping Communities" in a few weeks in a multi-aged first- and second-grade classroom. Evan displays a concept web of his unit plan and then discusses the background knowledge of mapping he has collected to date. Included in his sketch are children's books he has found useful. For one of his science investigation lessons, he will use magnets and compasses to teach map directionality.

Peers gather around to listen and help him shape his unit. Nikki asks, "Have you thought about three-dimensional house pieces from a game like Monopoly so your second-graders can have a concrete experience as they discuss the location of their homes to the school?" It becomes obvious to me that some students are beginning to think about developmental theories and the appropriateness of their planning for the children they are teaching. Anna suggests that he might consider asking children to make a map and write directions to a place in the school and then invite other children to try it. He considers and later adapts this peer suggestion.

I participate when needed and ask, "Evan, what is your guiding question? What is it that you want your students to know by the end of this unit?" Evan clarifies that his unit objective is for students to be able to read and make a basic map. Now I see that he is focusing his unit solely on the development of map skills and ask him to consider the bigger picture of mapping communities—location, spatial interaction, and internal structure of a city—while also teaching map skills. We hear each other's comments, but Evan will ultimately be responsible for shaping his final unit.

Pair and Cohort Mediation

Dyad and cohort work, dialogues in roundtables, and jigsaw and poster session formats are a norm in my teaching. Self and peer feedback and assessment are included in each experience. Mia, a graduate student, claims:

> I received continual support from my classmates. Sometimes the support was formal, such as the Author's Chair, and sometimes it was informal, such as someone suggesting a resource I might tap for more information. I also found it

helpful just to hear how other peoples' units were progressing; to find out that some were having the same problems I was; how others had overcome their problems. My peers gave me confidence, my professors gave me logistical guidance for the unit, and my cooperating teacher offered me materials [and] her knowledge about the unit topic, teaching upper elementary school students, and what was developmentally appropriate.

I have used the Internet to create more opportunities for peer mediation for my students. I have created an on-line discussion forum for the class, and I have located other on-line discussion groups that might provide support for them. There have been Web-based discussions to encourage interactive dialogue on such topics as whether it is appropriate for young children to learn about the Holocaust or about case studies about how to work with parents who don't think it's important for their daughter to pursue higher learning. Preservice teachers share journals of their field observations and reflections with peers and professors, both electronically and in seminars. I try to engage them in experiences they might enact with their own class, such as student-led book club meetings using social studies readings and thinking questions that require everyone to participate. Student evaluations have indicated that they learn easily from their peers. Preservice teachers have co-researched children's (and their own) science misconceptions. They have co-planned and co-taught science investigations for the class and conducted and presented their cooperative research.

As Wells (2000) notes, it is not necessarily the most expert who are able to share their expertise or assist the newcomer's induction or, in this case, entrance into the teaching profession. Drawing upon multiple sources of assistance provides multiple opportunities within multiple zones of proximal development to reach new understandings through others. The learner's attempts to explain their ideas to someone else may help them make more sense of it. Since collaborative does not mean the same thing as harmonious, the interaction may make them question their position or those of others as they develop new understandings (see Dillenbourg 1999). Throughout my teaching, I continuously create multiple layers and levels of participation in collegial communities of inquiry that include peers, professors, and cooperating teachers (see Figure 5.1).

Shadowing

Preservice teachers have opportunities to "shadow" science teachers and special education experts in their practicum schools. I tell them, "Get inside their heads and ask them what they are thinking when something is happening." Preservice teachers attend school functions such as back-to-school nights with their cooperating teachers and sit in on parent conferences when permitted. I use instructional formats of collective cognition to build professional relationships among peers through group and partner observation projects and to encourage my students to challenge their own thinking.

Poster Sessions

As we close our year together, preservice teachers participate in a poster session presentation of their unit outgrowth and write of their changed conceptions in a planning paper. I decided to use poster sessions so they could professionally present their work and allow their peers to hear their thinking about planning. In a videotaped recording of a poster session, Jody commented:

> I believe the planning cannot really be separated from the actual implementation, especially in reflective teaching, where what is learned from each step helps to make the next step better.

Kathleen remarked:

> Over the course of the past semester, I've come to realize that planning a unit does not mean planning one activity after another. My prior beliefs were that the formation of a unit was much like placing one block on top of another until the creation reaches a height that is believed to be satisfactory to the instruction. Now however, I see planning to be more like playing with Legos…[One needs] a firm base through activation of prior knowledge and interest [that is] geared toward the students at their own level of comprehension.

As I reflect on how on a technical level how I structured social mediation, I note that ideas have come easily to me. The Author's Chair exercise, using pairs and cohorts, shadowing assignments, and poster sessions are only a few of the activities I have designed. I look back through my syllabi and see how many ways I have used collective cognitive formats coupled with self-reflection. When I reflect on an interpretive level what this type of learning has meant to my students and how they have perceived it, I see that it has supported their thinking about teaching. We learn so much from each other, but I often get carried away with my enthusiasm. My students always say I give them too much. I do. I have dropped many assignments, but it seems that as soon as I let go of one idea, another comes to me. I have to always step back and evaluate if I am asking too much. I'm always working on challenging them in a balanced way; I focus equally on their learning and their development. On a critical level of reflection, I believe that I should push my students to expand their zones of proximal development, and I find that, just as Vygotsky theorized, their learning leads their development (see Figure 2.2). It is a very rewarding process to watch.

❖ Chapter 6
Learning Zones

Vygotskian Principle 4.
Education leads development.

Vygotsky's concept of the zone of proximal development (ZPD) is central to his theory of the development and mediation of higher psychological processes. The ZPD is defined as "the distance between the actual developmental level as determined by independent problem solving and the level of potential development as determined through problem solving under adult guidance or in collaboration with more capable peers" (Vygotsky 1978, 85). Vygotsky's tenet of the transfer of interpsychological to intrapsychological knowledge intrigues me, especially as it relates to the mediation of cognition. I later read about how the affective qualities of the relationship between teacher and student, as they relate to Vygotsky's theory, are considered to be an important component of cognitive development (Goldstein 1999). Effective instruction occurs when it proceeds ahead of, or leads, development, thus awakening those functions that are in the process of maturing within a ZPD. Outcomes are not predetermined but vary with the individual, with motivating factors, with assessment, and with the resources made available to the learner.

Proceeding ahead of the learner's development requires the mentor to raise the ante, at times to withdraw support and then proceed ahead with adjusted supports. The instruction is not linearly progressive or straightforward but is contingent upon the learner's feedback and comprehension. The more capable other enters a learner's zone or bandwidth of competence and encourages the learner to step beyond the edge of known skills, consequently nourishing what has yet to be seen or fully developed, such as problem-solving strategies. Strategy makes work easier, and others who are more capable than the learner in the area of strategizing can help the learner acquire that skill. This is not unlike what might be seen when a parent teaches a child how to tie their shoes, ride a bicycle, or construct a puzzle. I learned many of my strategy-making skills as I worked in our family restaurant.

Unfortunately, my part-time graduate studies didn't maximize opportunities to learn easily from others. I chose a part-time route since I insisted on also teaching part-time and being with my children. I have no regrets about those choices, but I sure used a lot of trial-and-error practice to figure out things the hard way. It's no surprise that I chose a doctoral study to investigate children who received help developing strategies with adult mediation and children who received no such mediation. A 4-year-old boy talks about his seemingly successful trial-and-error approach as he solves a puzzle on a computer program:

> Oops [inserts incorrect piece]. No [inserts incorrect piece]. This is what I regular[ly] do so I know what, where it goes. [Using one hand, he presses the piece selection key without looking through the selection and then immediately presses the space bar to insert the piece.] Some of them won't go in at all. [Now using two hands, the child rocks his upper body synchronically with the key presses. He moves more quickly as the probability of choosing the wrong piece lessens. Choosing an incorrect piece, he shouts out:] No way José! (Samaras 1996, 134)

The more effective instruction was to have the teacher use a nonlinear approach of moving ahead a few steps and then retracing old steps as needed. By attending carefully to students' statements, the teacher could more easily identify the child's understanding and adjust questioning accordingly, as in this puzzle-solving example:

Lola:	Now what are we doing?
Teacher:	Remember where you are now. See Snoopy sitting here on the red dog house?
Lola:	You mean he's sitting on the dog house and we're supposed to do that piece?
Teacher:	Yes.
Lola:	Now where are we looking or what piece are we looking for? [murmurs to herself] I'm looking for her hair.
Teacher:	Oh, we're down here. [Teacher points to the segment of the divided-puzzle that is not a piece of a character's hair.]
Lola:	Let me see something. [Child now looks back at the model independently] (Samaras 1996, 135)

For preservice teachers, learning occurs through the help of others, including peers, professors, and cooperating teachers, in a spiraling construction and reconstruction of knowledge. More capable others can share strategies and assist learners within their ZPDs. Strategy makes work easier, and others who are more capable than you in the strategy can help you learn it, especially because of differing gifts and overlapping ZPDs. Some have called this phenomenon "scaffolding."

Logbook, 20 September 1999

My attention is always drawn to scaffolding structures around the buildings in Washington, D.C., where I work, because they remind me of my first professional consulting job in 1990, which I called "Scaffolds." In this freelance work, I offered support systems for Head Start teachers through floor training, guided observation, and clinical supervision. I marvel at the scaffolding structure surrounding the Washington Monument or the National Shrine of the Immaculate Conception on the beautiful grounds of The Catholic University of America. When I read about the 750-ton scaffolding structure that literally supports the old facades of the Investment Building on 15th and K Streets NW, I was reminded of the difficulty with the term "scaffolding" in educational circles.

Scaffolds are typically erected to provide access for those who work on a building. There are also internal scaffolding structures for hard-to-reach places inside buildings. According to my son Gus, who is a civil engineer, scaffolds don't usually have anything to do with structural support. On the contrary, they allow the workers a way up and down the structure before there are stairs. Although the scaffold supports the workers, it does not typically support the building as it does with the Investment Building, whose old facades must be kept intact until the new building can support them. (It's actually a truss.)

So who are the scaffolds for in teacher education? Are they for teacher educators to gain access to preservice teachers' thinking about teaching? Are they erected by teacher educators to support preservice teachers until they can create their own inner and outer structural supports and no longer need the supports? I think they are both. In a way, they serve as a tool to conquer an evolving project, such as teaching and teaching teachers.

I have come to understand scaffolding as a nonlinear landscape for assessment that involves varying levels of scaffolding, de-scaffolding, and re-scaffolding within preservice teachers' ZPDs. It's like trying to fine-tune a hard-to-reach channel that isn't coming in quite clear enough on the radio. You might find it for a while and then lose it again and have to adjust it. Of course, some channels will be crystal clear or will come in better than others, at least temporarily. The key is to listen carefully and be attentive to small and significant changes over time.

"Scaffolding," a metaphor associated with working within a learner's ZPD, is a process of guided practice in which a tutor controls elements of a task that are initially beyond the learner's capacity (Wood, Bruner, and Ross 1976). Gradually, responsibility is shifted from joint problem-solving to independent problem-solving as the learner's mastery of the task increases. Wood and Wood (1996) discuss how the teacher supports the student's work toward self-regulation by providing sensitive help that is appropriate to the learner's knowledge, sharing strategies for learning, and encouraging the learner to take over subsets of the task when they are ready to do so. It is important for mentors to assess the demands of the task in the context of the skills of the apprentice and to structure the task so that the apprentice is constantly increasing his or her skill level. Mentors should also encourage the apprentice to reflect on their performance and to articulate what they are doing; this activity helps mentors assess the knowledge of the apprentice. Ideally, the teacher will model new strategies and intervene selectively as the learner experiments with a task. Selective intervention includes general verbal encouragement, specific verbal encouragement, selection of components of a task, preparation and presentation of material, and demonstration as necessary and contingent upon the learner's errors. Greenfield (1984) also discusses the selective and nonlinear use of scaffolding in everyday non-school tasks.

Unfortunately, scaffolding may become confused and equated with quantity or increments of assistance instead of qualitative shifts that lead to the learner's development (Bivens 1990; Samaras 1990a; Stone 1985; Tharp and Gallimore 1990; Wertsch 1984). I often hear teachers comment that they must move children *through* their ZPD. The learner doesn't necessarily transcend a zone. With effective instruction within the zone, the learner moves to the upper limits of the ZPD, thus creating an altered and adjusted ZPD. There is always a new zone to move within that likely has some of the upper boundaries still under development.

This process by which a child learns bears resemblance to how preservice teachers learn as beginners in their professional environment. They need support *during* problem-solving, and they also need to be paired with a more capable person who challenges the level of their existing skills within the particular situation with sensitivity to the preservice teacher's developmental level. Although preservice teachers struggle to make connections between the formal scientific knowledge acquired in textbooks and education courses and the situation they are in, they must also recognize that learning about teaching is ongoing.

Because of the heterogeneous nature of classrooms, including education methods classrooms, not only are there overlaps in core knowledge, but one person's ZPD may overlap with the core knowledge of others (see Hansen, Dirckink-Holmfeld, Lewis, and Rugelj 1999). (See Figure 6.1, where the ZPD is the outer rim and the center of the rim is core knowledge.) This will be similar to the school teaching teams in which they will one day work. When there is a collective core knowledge, the partner, his or her peers, his or her professors, and the cooperating teacher can each provide scaffolding for the preservice teacher within a distributive model of intelligence. Ideally, the cooperating teacher, education professors, and content professors should be sharing expertise among themselves and with preservice teachers such that there are in essence multiple and overlapping ZPDs.

What of this notion of overlapping ZPDs? What do we gain from working with people who are not like us? Can we learn from each other's strengths or gifts? Not everybody cares about the same things. That doesn't make them better than others. It gives them "differing gifts" (Keirsey and Bates 1984). A teacher's job is to find that gift and use it as an entry point to the student's learning. I try to recognize God's gifts, because our differing gifts are our gifts to each other. We are each uniquely shaped by our particular circumstances. If we look for the good in each other, we will always find something. We will also find that others can do things better than us, and we can learn from them. The most fortunate of us have had one of our gifts recognized by a teacher. I was reminded of this lesson recently when I saw a portrait exhibit at the Maryland Hall for the Creative Arts in Annapolis. Teachers need to be like good portrait artists, who in their brief exchanges with others come to know and portray the unique qualities of each student so that each student can share their unique gifts with others in the class. Another aspect of this role is that teachers can help the preservice teacher identify special talents that they might not have recognized. When teachers see only bodies of students instead of faces and characters, they have missed out on great teaching opportunities.

Self-Study Reflection

I developed an appreciation of the gifts of others at the restaurant. Each was educated in something more than I was, and I learned to respect that each one was a specialist and that I could learn from them. Over time, I recognized that each person has a gift and is worthy of respect, regardless of their background, despite the value society places on their worth. It's what makes us beautiful. Everyone matters. The employees were quite diverse and were very interesting people, not only in their unique skills but in their varied backgrounds. For example, one employee grew up on a farm, one was a college student and aviator, and another was a former convict. Some were illiterate or had limited academic skills, although waitresses could add checks in ways I hadn't learned about in school.

Miss Cheryl was very school-smart and because of that was given more business responsibility and a higher income. Because of her excellent math skills she was the bookkeeper for the restaurant. Mr. Charles was an expert at multitasking. He could be giving you tomorrow's menu, stirring a pot on the stove, and taking an order that someone just ran in and shouted—all at the same time. Miss Evelyn was such a gentle nonintrusive person. It was easy to confide in her and tell her my adolescent woes. As I learned of her family problems, I recognized that things don't always go the way you thought they would and that someone else's need could quickly take you in a different direction. Miss Cathy was a strategist with great interpersonal skills. She could really read her audience and know just how long her customers wanted her to hang around and talk, which always landed her a big fat tip. Some customers wanted more than food when they came to the restaurant.

Many of the employees had spent most of their lives in the south, some were from the north, and a few were transient. Most had worked at the restaurant for 15 to 20 years; two had worked there for 30 years. At my father's funeral, the priest made note of the loyalty of the restaurant employees and said it was a sign that my father had been good to them. He was fair and didn't ask them to do anything he wouldn't do himself. My father could be found cooking, clearing tables, trying to fix the dishwasher, or working the dumbwaiter that fell on his leg and contributed to his disability. I was watching him through all that and was finally able to see his gifts despite the things that bothered me about him.

Teachers are in a unique position to notice what each student brings to their class, which in turn can enrich the whole class. The student's gifts and interests can also be used as an entry point for teachers to extend that student's learning. Personally, I think most teachers have understood that students have multiple intelligences or differing gifts but have had to work within the restraints of mandated curriculums that typically do not capitalize on tapping into students' individuality. I found great value in trying to know my students' gifts. When the gift is recognized, the relationship between the teacher and student begins. To promote respect of differing gifts, I engage preservice teachers in many collaborative arrangements so they may share their gifts. I continue to do the same for myself,

Working in a small department limits my opportunities to learn new strategies and be a part of a distributive and collective core, so I have ventured outside the Department of Education. I also seek out joint ventures for myself. I try not to be discouraged about the competitiveness that typically permeates college campuses, where each professor boasts only their own specialty. I am bothered that some people can be too selfish to do what's good for the whole, but I decided that I needed to pay attention to what I was doing and not let the actions of others influence my actions. I have hungrily sought out new professional relationships because I want the challenge of learning outside of teacher education so I can see inside the worlds of other. I do not want to become stagnant or be locked into a routine. I always find myself restless for new projects that will push me outside my comfortable boundary. I want to feel a little nervous so I may be open to what emerges from my learning and teaching. My loyalty to the university as a professor and team player has led me to many cooperative efforts across campus; this has allowed me to recognize others' gifts in their respective disciplines. I have found a few good mentors who have been my lamplighters; they have gifts I don't have and are willing to share them with me.

Ways of Working Within Learning Zones

Logbook, 9 February 1998

A colleague's daughter graduated from college, got a job, and moved away from home. She is an independent woman but had never been solely responsible for her cooking or laundry. I suddenly feared the same fate for my daughter. Had I given her enough responsibility in household tasks? Had I sheltered her from the realities of survival or what Thomas (1985) calls "the torpedo's touch"? He notes: "In teaching we are too often persuaded to be gentle, fearing that we shall damage our children if we immerse them in dissonance or perplexity...We may argue that the young need not be torpified, but on the contrary require clarity, structure, simplification, reward. In their struggle to patch together the shreds of their identities, they reach out to us for guidance that we dare not withhold" (222).

Like Thomas, I don't want to lie in wait for schools to deliver the torpedo's touch to my students and shake them all at once. We can't coddle preservice teachers by keeping them on the sidelines in their first years of teacher preparation. They need early and continuous teaching responsibilities. Student teachers typically only have three weeks of full-time teaching responsibility and then are thrown into the spectator arena in their first year of teaching. No wonder there is such a serious attrition rate among new teachers.

Similarly, I can't tell my young daughter that she is now fully in charge of her cooking and cleaning, but I can't make her forever dependent on my support to complete the tasks. Just as with preservice teachers, she needs scaffolding early on with more gradual involvement but also with a letting go, or what I call de-scaffolding.

As a professor, I thought about how scaffolding applies to the process of learning to teach. As with young learners, teacher educators and cooperating teachers can interpret, remark upon, and extend preservice teachers' abstract thinking and help them develop problem-solving strategies. Teacher education programs need to include varying levels and degrees of assessment that enable others to scaffold and de-scaffold preservice teachers within their ZPD. Re-scaffolding is essential to encourage preservice teachers' lifelong learning.

Preservice teachers can work with a more capable other—peer, a professor, a cooperating teacher—to awaken the components of teaching that are in a process of developing. In assembled spaces such as in dyads and cohorts, they share their differing gifts and hear each other's expertise through dialogue. In that space, they will likely be able to replace inadequate strategies with those mediated by someone who is more experienced in a particular strategy. With others, they discover that the collective core knowledge is greater than that of the individual and that they can benefit from the combined potential if they can work together to formulate the problem, cooperate to find the solution, and collectively articulate the goal toward which they are working (see Hansen, Dirck-inck-Holmfeld, Lewis, and Rugelj 1999). When I use pairs in the shared task of the unit, they are working in the context of a goal-directed activity while also working in an interpretive zone toward a mutual understanding of the task. Together, their overlapping and unsettled knowledge is modified in a dynamic and intense exchange, but not without some conflict and incongruity (see Wasser and Bresler 1996). I think very seriously about what I do to support my students' construction of knowledge within their ZPDs. I consider the way class projects build upon previous projects and operate as foundations for later experiences in the program. Some of the ways I have used to work within preservice teachers' learning zones entail promoting learning communities, using formative assessment, and structuring research with peer feedback.

I strive to form communities where my students don't have to rely so heavily on trial-and-error techniques in learning to teach and where they can learn from others in a safe manner. I think of it as the part in the hide-and-seek game when someone shouts, "All-ee, all-ee in free!" because at that moment it's safe to come home without being called out or getting caught. Below is a log on my thinking about the need for a support system for preservice teachers to help them discover who they are as teachers before the student-teaching experience:

Logbook, 2 September 1997

We hopped on the metro rail to return to campus after our visit with a cooperating teacher at a practicum school site and sat in the front car. The ride was different from the usual ride. A feeling of danger overcame us as the car jerked and zigzagged. Then we heard conversation that verified our uncertainty. "That's it. Here it comes. Pass slowly. You've got it." The coaching helped us realize that the driver was new at this job. The car stopped suddenly and the coach left. We watched her grow smaller and smaller as the car pulled away. It seemed such a short and insignificant lesson. The driving suggested to us that the coaching was insufficient. Now the driver continued the job alone—carefully and with much hesitation. Our stop was next. We were glad to be getting off but we asked ourselves, "Is this what it's like for the preservice teachers we teach? Is the 14-week student-teaching experience substantial enough for their solo drives? Would learning and problem-solving with others, in the context of teaching tasks, help them know the dimensions of teaching?"

Learning Communities

For field experiences, I pair two preservice teachers with a cooperating teacher in a practicum so they can have an opportunity to learn what Lave and Wenger (1991) call the newcomer's tasks in "legitimate peripheral participation." I organize them in clusters in schools with other peers and cooperating teachers. Through situated learning in a school community and through shared cognitive experiences with peers and their cooperating teachers, they come to define for themselves what it means to be a teacher as they attempt to learn how to teach. One of my major teaching goals is to promote a co-mentoring relationship during the preservice teaching experience so they will learn to welcome the value of exchanging gifts and receiving constructive feedback. I ask them to redefine their earlier notions of mentoring, which are typically more appropriate for relationships between experts and novices or for remedial tutoring. This is particularly crucial for early childhood and elementary teachers, who require a broad knowledge base to teach many subjects. I use the Myers-Briggs Type Indicator (Briggs and Briggs Myers 1991) to code preservice teachers' learning preferences and teaching temperaments.

I explain to my students that I pair them according to their contrasting temperament styles, or what Keirsey and Bates (1984) call temperaments in teaching, in the second semester so they may capitalize on each other's strengths. I have observed that when partners differ about strategies and judgment, there is a greater probability that each partner will change his or her thinking and make greater individual progress. This method has been relatively successful unless the stretch is too large. Some preservice teachers initially feel uncomfortable about their differences, and a few were unable to overcome them. Nonetheless, the shared task of planning a unit requires them to listen to each other's points of view and thus promotes their reconstructive knowledge. Christine writes: "The cooperative effort was a challenge before we entered our practicum placement. We learned to work together, compromise our styles, and pool our resources to make this semester as fruitful as possible."

Formative Assessment

Diagnostic assessment is crucial in working within learning zones. Vygotsky was considered to be a "veritable virtuoso in diagnosing children" (Valsiner and van der Veer 2000). The learner, not just the subject matter, is at the heart of teaching. Students negotiate in their own minds what they understand as they seek to answer their own questions. Gibran (1923) speaks to us of teaching and learning and states, "No man can reveal to you aught but that which already lies half asleep in the dawning of our knowledge" (62). I consider this in terms of Vygotsky's ZPD. Teachers are the assessors of what students are trying to figure out. They do that first through the students' engagement in their own questions.

Preservice teachers need time for self-assessment of their new knowledge. What assessment procedures are in place to give immediate and contingent feedback on preservice teachers' performance? Think about when you go to the doctor's office. Now visualize that the doctor has examined you, given you a diagnosis, and recorded observations into a tape-recorder or in your file. That record of analysis and diagnosis of your condition will be available the next time you visit. Ideally, teacher educators should also have time to make ongoing assessments of their students' learning.

The interdisciplinary unit includes formative assessment throughout the semester by peers, the cooperating teacher, and professors (see Figure 6.2). Each assignment embedded in the interdisciplinary unit is considered in draft form, which allows the cooperating teacher, peers, and myself to discuss misconceptions or difficulties as they arise. There are due dates for all this preliminary work so I have the opportunity to provide continuous feedback and to mediate time management of tasks in teaching. I offer rewrites for assignments, especially lesson plans, with my comments and ask my students to resubmit their work as many times as needed. I give numerical points, and each assignment may be improved upon for final unit submission. Once I set a high level of expectation and return students' incomplete work, they tend to put more effort in their subsequent first submissions. Summative assessment moves beyond technical knowledge; it includes a self-evaluation and post-enactment evaluation of the unit, the integrity of the introductory material, the goals and sequence of activities, the authenticity of the lessons, and the existence and appropriateness of activities for content areas.

Research Paper with PDR

Preservice teachers have continuously commented that the research paper is one of the best projects that allows them to capitalize on other's strengths and compensate for their areas under development in their ZPDs. In the first professional semester, I ask my students to write a research paper on a curriculum dilemma that they have observed in the practicum classroom or one they have experienced themselves in their own schooling. They must first examine why they care about this subject; I often find that their interest links back to their education-related life history on such topics as pull-out programs, gender inequity, undemocratic classrooms, or learning disabilities. In their research papers, they talk about the dilemmas involved, the emotions the topic stirs up, and what action they would take if they were "in charge."

Later in the semester, they conduct a micro-teaching lesson for the class on a segment of their research findings using a teaching model (or models) they have learned about through a jigsaw activity. Jigsaw (Aronson 1997) is an approach to cooperative learning used in children's classrooms. I have adapted it to teacher preparation. I begin by assigning preservice teachers to research groups as they help each other research and study a model of teaching. After they learn their material, they are mixed with peers in other learning groups, and each one teaches their peers about the teaching model they researched. Since they are the only ones that have researched that teaching model, each team has become an expert on their own topic. Preservice teachers submit a post-enactment reflection and self-evaluation of their micro-teaching lesson that incorporates peer evaluations. I use the jigsaw approach so preservice teachers can learn teaching models. I also use it so they can experience its collaborative and cognitive value and consider using it with their own students. I found that many choose to use it in their own teaching during the practicum and later during their student-teaching experience.

During the early development and draft stage of the research paper, preservice teachers present and dialogue their beginning sketches with a peer for feedback and revision. I have titled this activity PDR I—Present, Dialogue, and Revise. They discuss research directions and receive peer feedback during the paper's development. Later in the semester, after researching the topic further and collecting more data from the field site, the dyad meets again and repeats the exercise in PDR II. I have also used interactive roundtables of related research topics for students' informal presentations.

I also ask that they propose ideas for action research based on their literature review and field observations. This is an important forerunner and foundation for the development of an actual research paper that they complete during student teaching, which is also their comprehensive examination. At that time, they will not only tell about their ideas for action but also act and reflect upon them after thoroughly considering the consequences of their choices.

Present, Dialogue, Refine (PDR I & II)

The following is the PDR format I developed to promote collective cognition while peers work within multiple ZPDs:

Find a peer who is sitting across the room from you that you have never worked with before. Each of you will present the beginning sketches of your research paper. You will have an opportunity to repeat this exercise later in the semester (PDR II).

- Tell your peer the intent of your paper in one sentence. Your peer will tell you if your intent is clear, vague, too broad, or too narrow.
- Begin to explain in more depth now what your paper will cover using your rough outline as a guide. Your peer will stop and question you when there is ambiguity or where your intent in no longer clear.
- Your peer will offer suggestions, redirection, and refinement. Write down the peer's suggestions and a plan of action for any needed edits.
- Explain your typical research process and the writing process you employ and listen to your peer's approach.
- Submit your work next week with a new working outline.
- Reverse roles and do the process again with your peer's research.

On a technical level of reflection, I have found that learning communities, formative assessment, and peer feedback for research projects are excellent ways to work within preservice teachers' learning zones. On an interpretive level of reflection, preservice teachers begin to understand that learning is a complicated and sophisticated process and that we can learn with the constructive feedback of others. I hope they take that message with them and reflect upon it often in their own classrooms. On a critical level of reflection, when I ask myself the question why this notion of learning zones is so important to teaching preservice teachers, I see the faces of my students who, just like children, do not all develop at the same rate. They too deserve attention to their unfolding levels of maturation as they learn to teach (see Figure 2.2).

As I discuss throughout this book, I place great emphasis on the need for preservice teachers to be supported in their fieldwork and coursework prior to the student-teacher experience. The program situates its curriculum to support the entry of preservice teachers into a professional teaching community. Professors, peers, and cooperating teachers each play a supportive role in the transition from preservice teacher to student teacher.

I have been collecting data on this curriculum for almost a decade to investigate preservice and cooperating teachers' perceptions of their experiences in this intentional curriculum. In both their written course evaluations and exit interviews, preservice teachers repeatedly comment on how they applied what they learned in coursework to the practicum and how they adapted it to fieldwork. They indicate that the integrated unit, although most demanding, helps them connect the theory with the practice. Although they still comment that practice matters most, they also talk about their own applications of what they learned at the university and the implications of their teaching for their students.

I watch my students change and grow professionally over time as they become more knowledgeable and confident about their teaching actions. I read in their reflective journals about their growing awareness that each child is unique and that many have problems they can't handle. I find that most preservice teachers have learned to accept their teaching mistakes as part of a continuous learning process. In professional growth papers, they report that they are willing to view themselves critically through reflection in an effort to improve their pupil's learning. Most developed an incredible sense of their students' individual differences. Some have learned how to individualize and adjust their teaching accordingly as they read their classroom audience. In progress reports, preservice teachers write about the cognitive support they received from peers, cooperating teachers, and professors; they especially appreciate the emotional and collegial value of planning and teaching with others. The situated learning allowed them to improve and caused them to think about real classrooms.

They improved by seeing not only what to do but what not to do. Watching ineffective teachers verified what they did not want to be like as teachers. Working in poorly run schools allowed them to see the broader institution of schooling, the effects of mismanagement, and the children who consequently suffer because of it. At the end of our year together, they talk about the realities and struggles they experienced by actually being in the classroom. They are glad they had each other. And to think some of them once thought that teaching was an easy profession.

Part III. Case Studies Using a Vygotskian Approach

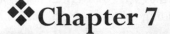

Chapter 7

Redefining the Mentor

In Greek mythology, Odysseus leaves his family to fight in the Trojan War and entrusts his son, Telemachus, to Mentor, who is responsible for educating, guiding, protecting, and leading him toward independence and good decision-making. Who is the mentor for teachers? Is it the "excellent" cooperating teacher? Who might that be? Can there be multiple mentors for different purposes? This is a case study that redefines mentors as peers who work with cooperating teachers and professors.

Two elementary education undergraduate majors, both Caucasian females, were assigned to teach in a fourth-grade classroom with a veteran teacher who is also Caucasian and female. The public elementary school includes pre-kindergarten through sixth-grade classes and has approximately 400 students. It is considered to have one the best inclusive curriculums in the district. Children whose families work in nearby embassies give the school an international composition. At the time of the study, the racial composition was 75 percent Caucasian, 13 percent African-American, 8 percent Hispanic, and 4 percent Asian-American. The school has a progressive and child-centered curriculum with multi-aged groupings. Students are viewed as active participants in their learning and are given opportunities to search for answers to the questions they pose. Teams of teachers work on school and grade-level improvement measures and continuously discuss and assess each student's progress. Teachers can be found integrating subjects such as science, social studies, and art as they teach content, skills, and the interconnections across disciplines. They teach about topics such as the rainforest, water, or the Renaissance, centered on concepts such as interdependence, conservation, and discovery, respectively. State-of-the-art computer programs are a part of classroom instruction; for example, students conduct surveys of local pollution problems and then share and compare their results with students in another country. It is a lively school where children work on large projects in the hallways and on floors. It is not unusual to see groups of children learning outdoors, going on field trips, or attending school assemblies.

The second triad also consisted of two elementary education under-graduate majors, both Caucasian females, who were assigned to teach in a first-grade classroom with a teacher who is also Caucasian and female. This parochial school includes grades one through eight and enrolls approximately 200 students from all parts of the city. At the time of this study, the school's racial composition was 50 percent African- Ameri-can, 35 percent Caucasian, 12 percent Hispanic, and 3 percent Asian-American. It is a quiet place with many rules. Students are constantly patrolled in the hallways. In this first-grade classroom, students sit in orderly rows; there are no learning centers. The school was working on schoolwide themes of self-worth, care, and respect with a progressive principal who was working on restructuring the curriculum in the context of a more traditional faculty.

You are now familiar with the university program context and the coursework and fieldwork structures. For this research, data sources included:

a. one-on-one audiotaped semi-structured interviews conducted with preservice and cooperating teachers
b. videotaped presentations of preservice teachers' poster format sessions of their unit planning
c. papers preservice teachers wrote of their education-related life histories
d. papers preservice teachers wrote about planning that included their pre-planning and post-planning concept maps of their notions of planning
e. papers preservice teachers wrote about their professional growth
f. the field progress reports of the preservice teachers
g. the self-evaluation papers of the preservice teachers
h. papers preservice teachers wrote about their background knowledge, including pre-planning and post-planning concept maps of their subject knowledge
i. weekly reflective journals the preservice teachers e-mailed to professor
j. mid-term and final self-evaluations by the preservice teachers

k. mid-term and final evaluations of the preservice teacher by the cooperating teacher

l. the interdisciplinary unit the preservice teacher constructed and taught, including his or her self-evaluation of the unit

I read and re-read preservice and cooperating teachers' reports, making remarks and memos in the margins. I compared and contrasted repeated statements with other statements across the data, which allowed me to analyze for patterns of similarities and differences and the marking preliminary categories. I sketched numerous matrixes and charts as a precursor to data displays (Miles and Huberman 1984) to obtain a visual gestalt. With assistance, the codes were operationalized and coding-checking for reliability was conducted. Once the key categories were identified, I reanalyzed the data more systematically using a first-level analysis that involved a line-by-line coding. Pattern coding was used to group overarching themes or constructs of preservice teachers' views about the curriculum and to cluster their views across participants (Bogden and Biklen 1992). Continuous refinement and reduction of categories was conducted over the multi-data set.

The analysis resulted in three major themes that characterized preservice and cooperating teachers' perceptions of their learning experiences: (1) the importance of situating learning; (2) the importance of a sense of partnership/ownership for their teaching; and (3) the importance of feedback about their teaching and being given free rein while they did it (Samaras and Gismondi 1998). Here, I address the "so whats" of the research as they relate to our broad program goals and the support structures that I presented in Part I and Part II.

Situating Learning and Program Goal One

Program Goal One. Program Goal One is to provide preservice teachers with a coherent experience that will allow them to see the curriculum in action and the way learning experiences build upon learning experiences. In this study, preservice teachers seemed to gain experience as teachers by becoming accustomed to a school and coming to feel that they belonged to an actual classroom. They were able to use and situate their learning from methods courses, recognize when they were doing so, and acquire a better understanding of teaching. They connected theory to practice in numerous ways by trying out techniques in the environment of a particular grade and class. The classroom dynamics required them to reflect and take action in terms of integrating content, making the material their own, and revising plans, as the following preservice teacher's transcribed interview comment suggests:

> Irene: I learned a lot in classes, but writing lesson plans is more or less hypotheti-
> cal. I think actually implementing the unit, having to combine the strategies, the
> timing, the disciplines, [has been very helpful]. Before, everything was so sepa-
> rate. I would try to combine the disciplines, but it was all on paper. I wouldn't
> have had to [learn the executive, interactive, and organizational functions of
> teaching] without the unit and without the fieldwork.

Preservice teachers reported that teaching the unit taught them about how children think and how they process information for particular tasks. They came to know and assess children as individuals in a schooling context, noting that the diversity among learners was greater than they could ever have imagined. They learned to be comfortable with the different paces of students and their effects on the lessons and experimented with ways to motivate and manage classrooms in the practicum. As they faced dilemmas, they had to make decisions about the curriculum. In a Vygotskian sense, the authentic setting let them experience the concepts and theories, which they had only read about in textbooks, in action in a classroom. Alexis reflected:

> I learned a lot of what I learned in my classes in the [practicum] classroom. I
> learned a lot about heterogeneous and homogeneous groupings, and it helped me
> a lot. And I saw it working—that children can learn from one another. I think
> every day I pulled on my coursework. I have so many examples and it just all fell
> in together, at the end especially.

The situated learning also enabled preservice teachers to observe the impact of a particular school's curriculum, which for Gina and Ann contradicted what they were learning in the university culture. They expressed the dissonance they found in their context:

> Ann: I was shocked because Gina and I went in [the library] with the class when
> they had their library time, and they were looking at books, and they were talk-
> ing: "Look at the book I found!" And [the librarian] would just tell them to shut
> up. We were like "Oh no! Don't tell them to shut up. They're excited about it.". . .
> We would go to science class with our class, and I would sit in the back and just
> cry in my tea watching this woman teacher. I thought, "This is awful." She was
> shouting out answers and throwing candy at those who got them right and yelling
> at kids who weren't paying attention. I thought, "Oh God, no, this is awful."

Gina and Ann reflected deeply about numerous dilemmas having to do with control, the curriculum, and the social situations they observed within the classroom context. Gina and Ann realized that the practicum placement was not ideal with respect to the cooperating teacher's model of teaching. However, they repeatedly remarked that they gained a deeper understanding of the dynamics of a classroom, who they were becoming as teachers, and what might await them after graduation:

> Gina: It made us think. It gave us great journals. It makes me think a lot. Well, this is exactly what we learned not to do. How would I have done it?

> Ann: I learned many valuable lessons that I would not have learned at a more progressive school. I was forced to reflect upon how I would choose to handle the situation. I was forced to look at a deeper and personal level of understanding of how I plan to implement my lessons...This is the real world. I learned that the way our teacher taught works, but it just doesn't work the way that I want it to work. So I definitely know when I'm going into that and realize, well do I want to be teaching this way?

Partnership/Ownership and Program Goal Two

Program Goal Two. Program Goal Two is to give preservice teachers an opportunity to design and carry out a sequence of instruction. As a shared task (each set of partners completed one unit), the unit created a common ground for continuous communication and jointly mediated knowledge. Preservice teachers had to constantly discuss and assess their teaching with a peer, exchanging interpersonal knowledge about teaching—for example, sharing between people to enhance their intrapersonal knowledge—which they internalized to use later independently (Wertsch 1985).

The cooperating teachers spoke of the practicum partnership in contrasting ways. Ms. Athens described the preservice teachers as a support to each other and to her in the classroom. She capitalized on their areas of expertise and gave them individual assignments. She did not see them as a burden but viewed them "like having two other teachers in the room." Ms. Rose, on the other hand, felt that each member of the pair did not allow either one to have enough practice and that they made her nervous and self-conscious about her teaching.

The preservice teachers claimed that the partnership was not easy or comfortable but was beneficial to their learning. Some later adapted the partnership strategies in their own classrooms. The pairs of preservice teachers used each other as sounding boards to listen to their triumphs and disappointments and to sort out their observations as they questioned practice. The partnerships supported them in their beginning efforts to teach against the grain and to deal with dilemmas they knew they would soon encounter in the work world. The contrasts between theory and practice that Gina and Ann witnessed and shared appeared to strengthen and validate their own theories of teaching. They learned to compromise and go along with the cooperating teacher's methods, since it was her classroom and they were guests. Nonetheless, over time, Ann's obsequious manner was replaced with a less compliant one, especially when she was put in a situation that contradicted her teaching philosophy. This is evident in this statement:

> Ann: The first activity that I did with the kids was one-on-one tutoring, and she said, "Could you help Maggie?" and I said, "Sure." So I went to the back of the room and I said to her, "Would you like to sit in a chair or on the floor?" And Maggie said, "On the floor." So I said, "Okay," and I sat on the floor with her. The little girl looked at me like I was crazy, and Ms. Rose was not happy at all. She just looked at me like "How can you do that? You're on the floor! Get up." And I thought, I should get up, but I'm not [going to] because this is what Maggie wants. She's more comfortable down here. I'm staying down here. And then I realized that I had to—I did sort of change to fit her classroom. I'd sit on a small chair instead of on the floor. But I refused to sit at the desk while the child was on the floor.

Although, Irene and Alexis did not struggle to teach against the grain as did Gina and Ann, they became aware of the difficulties of other school realities in the practicum seminar when peers read journal reflections. In her self-evaluation paper, Alexis wrote:

> My goals as a teacher, after this experience, would be that you're not going to be in the perfect situation, but that's the whole thing. You have to be the difference and you have to make the situation—create a situation where learning takes place. I do want a job, but I'm going to have to teach how I learned to teach. I have to take what I learned here, and I'm not going to back down, and I know God is looking at all times to help me through that.

Classmates also served as partners when they helped mediate unit development in the Author's Chair activity and offered lesson revisions. Groups of preservice teachers carpooled to the practicum sites and met inside and outside of methods courses. Some came to be known as the "education groupies" at the college dining hall where they gathered to eat together and share their ordeals. One preservice teacher gave this assessment:

> We felt the strongest support we received for implementing our unit was from our peers. They always offered ideas, and knowing that they were going through similar experiences helped and motivated us. To work with others and succeed is the best feeling in the world. I learned more than ever how much support is needed.

My data supported the theory that the pairing fostered perspective-taking and required peers to learn negotiation strategies, with each other and their cooperating teachers. Preservice teachers saw negotiating as a necessary but difficult professional skill. They spoke of looking more critically at their views and actions as they attempted to articulate them to others. Although they complained about their differences in the beginning of the semester, over time they remarked that their way might not always be the best, or only, way. Gina explained the tensions and benefits of this double bind in her interview:

> I would have liked to do a unit by myself. Just because we're very different...We were a big complement for each other because she relaxed me and I got her on the ball a little bit. [We] definitely had different perspectives, which was good...And it's funny how we would interpret something that happened in the classroom. "Can you believe she did that?" [I would say]. Ann was like, "Yeah!" But Ann would have seen it in an entirely different way.

The pairs of preservice teachers felt both a sense of partnership in and a sense of individual ownership of their teaching. They co-planned, co-taught, and co-evaluated their efforts while they also individually developed, taught, and evaluated their own lessons. When lessons were implemented, either through team-teaching or individually, they offered and easily accepted each other's feedback. The practicum gave preservice teachers opportunities to plan, teach, and take responsibility for their work. They constructed knowledge about planning in the context of social interactions. One can sense the problem-solving, joint decision-making, and ongoing refinement in the unit construction in the following example:

> [The unit] seemed to shift the whole time. You think, okay, this is my unit. [But] it never goes straight. You always branch out. We branched out so many times. Let's do this. No, this might not go too well. They might not learn. It may be too difficult. Let's go this way.

In one triad, a sense of ownership was nested in a co-teaching relationship between peers and with the cooperating teacher. In the other triad, the peers learned to offer each other support when they saw it would not be forthcoming from their cooperating teacher. Through their mutual support and the constant support they received from their peers, they were able to feel successful in their teaching. In a peer evaluation, Ann stated:

> Gina's ability and maturity in the classroom is quite advanced. Over the course of the semester, she has helped me not only as a peer, but also as a mentor. Her composure and creativity are inspirational. Much of the success I've experienced in my lessons was a direct result of her assistance.

The way that ownership developed, however, was related to the role of the cooperating teachers and resulted in very different learning experiences. Cooperating teachers did not express any tensions about letting preservice teachers "do their own thing." However, they played different roles while preservice teachers tried the practices advocated in coursework. The difference in support preservice teachers received from their cooperating teachers is discussed in the third category, giving feedback/allowing free rein, which relates to the program goal three.

Giving Feedback
Allowing Free Rein and Program Goal Three

Program Goal Three. Program Goal Three is to give preservice teachers an opportunity to learn instructional techniques from cooperating teachers and try out practices advocated in coursework. Analysis of data from preservice and cooperating teachers indicated stark contrasts in the types of feedback cooperating teachers provided and the degree of free rein they gave preservice teachers in the classroom. Tharp and Gallimore (1990) point out that teachers, like children (Samaras 1991; Wood, Bruner, and Ross 1976), have ZPDs that require assisted performance. They list six ways to assist the performance of inservice teachers: modeling, contingency management, giving feedback, instructing, questioning, and structuring cognition. Giving feedback was identified as "the single most effective means of self-assistance" (54). I define feedback as the dialogue between individuals for correction that may lead to internalized self-regulation. Without meaningful feedback, the preservice teachers had little professional support as they "took over" the classroom. Cooperating teachers' feedback and the degree of free rein they offered were examined through the task of the unit, from its conception to completion: during planning, during development, during teaching, during assessment, and at the conclusion of the field experience.

Giving free rein is giving a preservice teacher full responsibility and control in the classroom. In the planning of the unit, Ms. Athens played a crucial yet nondirective role as a partner in the conception of the unit topic, in the early stages of its development, and in its long-term planning outline. As with her own students, she used the preservice teachers' interests and experiences as springboards for their learning. Although she pulled from their interests, she asserted that "it had to fit into what we were doing." She considered the unit to be essential to the ongoing curriculum. Ms. Rose allowed Gina and Ann total free rein to select the unit topic. As Gina remarked, it didn't have anything to do with what they were doing in the curriculum." Ms. Athens, unlike Ms. Rose, required mutual planning time, with dialogue about mapping out lesson sequence, objectives, and deadlines during the planning and development of the unit. Irene explained:

From the beginning, she forced us to figure out how we were going to organize [the unit]. She sat down with us. She did the very beginning of the planning. From there we were kind of on our own, but she helped in that, the long range planning...She wanted to know exactly what we were going to cover, when we were going to cover it, and how long it would take. She gives you so much freedom, so much time.

During the development of the unit, Ms. Athens considered the preservice teachers to be part of the classroom and appreciated the sharing of teaching responsibilities. Ms. Athens notes, "I got ideas from them and they got ideas from what I had done before. I think that really helped me." They met during her planning time, when she made sure everything was working. Ms. Rose offered little feedback during the development of the unit, and that frustrated Gina and Ann. When they heard of other preservice teachers' positive experiences during the practicum seminar, they said they felt cheated.

Ann: Really the only thing [Ms. Rose] worked with us [with regard to] the planning was we would ask her, "What do you plan on doing next week?" And she would have a list of the pages in the textbook that they were doing...Very often after we had something planned, we would go to her and ask, "Do you think this will work?"—Just to get her opinion. Once in a while she would suggest a change, then that would make it easier to implement in the classroom, and sometimes we said, "This is what we want to do, we need time."

In the teaching and assessment of the unit, both cooperating teachers "handed over the class" to the preservice teachers, but in very different ways. In many ways, the degrees of feedback and free rein the cooperating teachers offered the students was a reflection of their teaching styles and what they modeled in teaching their own students. The cooperating teachers needed to feel comfortable with the preservice teachers' "taking over" in the class, but in order to feel comfortable with that degree of autonomy, the preservice teachers needed feedback from the cooperating teachers. Ms. Athens came to know the preservice teachers and established a climate for them to learn from each other. Working within preservice teachers' ZPDs required Ms. Athens to talk with them and find out what they were interested in and what they knew. She needed to structure an entrance into teaching by offering gradations of teaching responsibility, giving specific feedback, and requiring reflective assessments of their coursework and fieldwork. From the outset, she gave the pair teaching time, encouraged them to take risks, and gave them a chance to try out what they had learned in courses while she was in the classroom. She commented:

> I divided my reading group right away for them and gave them six students each. They had to take care of those students; we talked about the books that we were reading. I talked about different activities that I had done, and I told them to come up with different activities that they enjoyed doing. I thought it was important they did what they had to do and what we were doing...I gave them a group and we built activities on our reading and I linked it to geography and creative writing. I asked them for suggestions.

Although Gina and Ann showed initiative in getting more involved in the classroom, Ms. Rose did not express confidence in their readiness to teach for any length of time. When they did teach, her feedback was general and she offered no ideas for improvement. Ms. Rose kept them mainly in the role of observer, tutor, and teacher's aide. She even controlled the classroom while they taught, as Ann noted:

> She definitely had control of the classroom at all times—even when I was teaching a lesson. This made it very difficult for me to work on my goal of becoming an effective disciplinarian. I wanted to try some of the techniques that I was

learning…The first times Gina and I did lessons, Ms. Rose sat behind us and said [to the children], "Sit on your bottom. Keep your mouth closed. If you have a question, put your hand up." You know, I felt like, "Just let them go. Leave them alone. They're first-graders."

Gina and Ann began to rely heavily on each other and on classmates for support. Although Ms. Rose said she wanted to use the feedback as some tool of guidance, she was never quite certain how that should be accomplished, so she left it more to chance, as is evident here:

Ms. Rose: Being my first time [with practicum students], I was just like "whatever you want to do." I didn't want to be, you know, I was just very open to whatever they wanted to do. I was confused with my role basically. I just kind of saw it, when the opportunity came up, that I could illustrate a point to them…I was not on them at all…I guess I just waited for them to come to me…We never actually sat down during one of my breaks and discussed things.

Without a balance of feedback and free rein, Gina and Ann had little professional support to help them learn how to control a class. At times when the class became chaotic as they taught, Ms. Rose would indicate that she knew their approach wouldn't work but she didn't say what would help. When they could teach, Gina and Ann did try out strategies taught in methods courses, but these were strategies to which the children were not accustomed:

Ann: Once when [the cooperating teacher] was gone for about a week, we had a substitute who let us do quite a few different things. And we tried to get the kids to do cooperative learning, which I did last semester. Then I tried it at St. John's, and it was a disaster. We put them in groups, and everybody had a job…and it ended up becoming a little fight in each group of kids. There was one group that worked together beautifully, and the rest had problems…At the end of the exercise, one of the little boys came up to me and said, "Could we not play that game again? It made my tummy ache."

After completing lessons, each preservice teacher wanted to know "How did I do?" Ms. Athens used feedback as a way to have preservice teachers self-analyze. She spent a lot of time with preservice teachers during the mid-term and final practicum evaluations. She often asked them to reconstruct their experiences and to think about what they thought they understood, and she encouraged them to reflect beyond the immediate environment. Alexis explained Ms. Athens's feedback style in the following statement:

> Alexis: I always asked her what she thought, and she would never tell me what she thought. She makes me be the critical thinker. Self-evaluation, that's her big—that's her key thing...She wanted me to self-analyze all the time, and I learned from that. I learned a lot.

At the conclusion of the unit, Ms. Athens noted in the final evaluations of Alexis and Irene that they planned a unit that focused on the needs and interests of each student and that it was evident that her students improved in reading comprehension, social studies, and art. Ms. Rose spoke of Gina and Ann's patience, caring, and gentleness in their final evaluations. She was surprised when Gina and Ann showed her the unit binder at the end of the semester, because she had no idea that they were actually doing that much work. Irene and Alexis stated in their interviews that they were "confident, not worried, and excited" about student teaching. In contrast, Gina and Ann felt they had grown, but not in a way that prepared them for student teaching.

> Ann: I'm scared [about student teaching]. I don't think I grew like I should have grown...I felt like I was really reinforcing everything that I had already learned because I was thinking about it all the time, but I wasn't learning new things...I definitely grew. I just grew in an entirely different way than I expected to grow.

Although one cannot make broad generalizations about the experiences my students had in this study, the issues they raised are important and have serious implications for teacher educators. First, this study exemplifies how action research and the self-study of that action research can inform the practice of teacher educators and the design of teacher education programs. According to Zeichner (1995), most academicians involved in teacher research pay little homage to the process of action research in school-based inquiry or in studying their own university-based teaching practices as a form of knowledge production. In that respect, the study demonstrates the value and legitimacy of action research and self-study in teacher education.

Second, the findings suggest that situated learning may benefit preservice teachers' understanding of planning, perspective-taking, social negotiation, and the importance of a sense of ownership of the material they teach. The Vygotskian-designed program enabled preservice teachers to experience authentic teaching with tasks that were shared between and among peers and a cooperating teacher. The multiple opportunities and structures for high levels of interaction may have facilitated the development of preservice teachers' sense of partnership and professional collegiality. Some cooperating teachers have communicated to us that they feel a professional responsibility to assist novices as they enter the profession of teaching. Maybe teacher educators need to instill that sense of collegiality in today's novices. Building collaborative mind-sets during professional training may help offset the problem of teacher isolation somewhat in the future.

Preservice teachers had opportunities to experience collective cognition—to construct knowledge in partnership with others in coursework and fieldwork. They were able to witness and experience the ways that theory becomes practice, to solve problems with others, and to make public their reflections in journals, a series of papers, exit conferences, and interviews. They expressed and sorted out their disappointments and confusion and the connections they made between what they read about in methods courses and what they actually experienced in the field. They certainly saw curriculum in action as they planned and tried out what they were learning in coursework and critically questioned practice. The experience appears to have led both pairs to a better understanding of teaching and helped bring practice closer to program goals.

Third, the study highlights the different support systems that preservice teachers can receive in practicum experiences. There were two collaborative relationships at work in this study—peer with peer and peers with cooperating teacher. I want to make two cautionary points. First, placing preservice teachers in cohorts or pairs is not all there is to a Vygotskian approach in teacher education. It involves a process of joint activity or a system of mediation where the individual develops skills within a social context and a shared definition of the task at hand. Second, the varying support systems that preservice teachers received from cooperating teachers indicate that preservice teachers cannot always rely on the support of their cooperating teachers. Over many years, we have found only a handful of cooperating teachers who conceptualize Vygotskian notions of teaching—understanding entry points for supportive feedback, when to assist or move forward with tasks of increasing difficulty. The support is not a planned sequence, nor is it linear; it is more like tacking while sailing, an activity that requires the teacher to pay close attention to changes in the context, work within the ZPDs of preservice teachers, and let them make their own small mistakes. Both cooperating teachers had blocks of time for informal exchange with preservice teachers before or after the learning experiences. However, only one of them used this time to work with the students.

At the beginning of the semester, a colleague and I met with both cooperating teachers to explain the program, provide model units, and clarify their roles. We made multiple school visits, reviewed weekly practicum liaison notes, and addressed concerns throughout the semester with preservice and cooperating teachers. Although we identified the effective scaffolding characteristics used by Ms. Athens, we did not help build a sense of trust between Gina, Ann, and Ms. Rose or between Ms. Rose and the university. On the other hand, the lack of a support system may have had less to do with building trust between people and more to do with cultural and institutional constraints. School systems are not always conducive to collaborative models.

Perhaps Ms. Rose felt obligated to work in unison with her school curriculum (although it was under serious revision). I have asked if her laissez-faire style had to do with her unfamiliarity with our program. It is not clear what factors inhibited her ability to serve as an effective mentor for Gina and Ann. While I gave much thought to the design for coursework and the support preservice teachers could receive, I paid less attention to working with the cooperating teacher. I need to think about how I can provide a supportive environment for both the preservice teachers and the cooperating teachers; I also need to examine the school environment in more depth. Unfortunately, the time and effort required to develop university-school partnerships is not always given or appreciated by schools and universities.

This study affirms my belief that practicum experiences need to provide formative assessment for preservice teachers. Lortie (1975) states that in most professional apprenticeships a "neophyte is ushered through a series of tasks of ascending difficulty and assumes greater responsibility as his technical competence increases...The circumstances of the beginning teacher differ...Tasks are not added sequentially to allow for gradual increase in skill and knowledge; the beginner learns while performing the full complement of teaching duties" (72). In contrast to what student teachers experience, these practicum students could focus on a task while observing the full complement of teaching in a specific school curriculum and classroom context. They could also receive feedback that would not penalize their chances of getting a job after graduation because of a poor evaluation from the cooperating or university supervisor. Ralph, Kesten, Lang, and Smith (1998) found that administrators place the highest value on evaluation reports and profiles of interns when they hire new teachers.

Fourth, this study reveals the need for more careful investigation of the professional and survival skills that best prepare preservice teachers for working in schools. Those skills include: (1) collaboration, particularly to help students cope with and persevere in a difficult situation; (2) negotiation about teaching responsibilities; and (3) reflections about teaching. Goodman and Fish (1997) also found that a crucial teaching skill is learning how to collaborate and negotiate with colleagues, especially with those in power and/or those who hold differing perspectives. We too strive, like Cochran-Smith (1991), Goodman and Fish (1997), and Short and Burke (1989), to place our preservice teachers with cooperating teachers who carefully examine their own practice and its impact on children's learning and who are willing to depart from current practices of the school if they are ineffective. However, since ideal cooperating teachers, field placements, and schools are not always available, learning professional collegiality will provide a modest shield for the battlefield ahead.

This study focused on preservice partnerships and the cooperating teacher's role in a practicum experience. It did not investigate the impact of the school environment on those relationships or look at curriculum in action from a broader perspective. The schools in this study certainly reveal fascinating contexts for future research. How did the cooperating teachers' accustomed ways of teaching influence the practicum experience and their role as mentor? Does a more rigid school schedule and framework make it more difficult for cooperating teachers to work within preservice teachers' ZPDs? Was there a fragmented schedule at St. John's School that hindered cross-disciplinary projects? How do school standards, curriculum requirements, and the physical environment affect the role of a cooperating teacher who is working with preservice teachers on an interdisciplinary unit?

The study also begs the old, yet unanswered, question, "Which schools are best to use to foster preservice teachers' professional growth and reflection?" When are field experiences educational? Field experiences remain a perplexing issue in teacher education. We want our preservice teachers to see "good" schools and do not want to expose them to any poor teaching models they might mimic. Unfortunately, working with good schools does not guarantee cooperating teachers who are able to demonstrate and mentor effective teaching. Furthermore, we have found that despite the advantages and consistency that typically are provided when working with the same schools over time, especially professional development schools, that stability is weakened by the transience of principals and teachers. This study painfully reminds me of the problematic nature of the practicum that teacher educators and their students often face. I would like to clearly note that the schools in this study are not representative of all public, private, or parochial schools we have utilized and that schools can change over time. Each school is unique.

We wonder if the ideal textbook model for a field placement prepares our preservice teachers for the real world of working in urban schools. As one preservice teacher commented, "I think we learned a lot [about] what it's going to really be like when we have jobs as teachers." Even in less-than-ideal practicum placements, learning through reflection can take place. It is not clear from this study why certain events are more meaningful than others. Negative experiences may provide insights and lead to critical reflection (Armaline and Hoover 1989; Treiber 1984). The seemingly ineffective field experience reaffirmed and legitimized Gina and Ann's beliefs as they began to see themselves as active creators in their own learning. Providing multiple and various field placements with support from peers and a cooperating teacher may offer preservice teachers opportunities for negotiation, deeper reflection, and validation of their beliefs about teaching. Peers can serve as the additional scaffolds preservice teachers need to support them as they learn to teach; sometimes peers may be the only support systems available. With few guarantees of what preservice teachers will encounter after graduation, peer scaffolding may ease some of the difficulty in learning to teach.

I recognize that there is a need for further research and understanding about sociocultural models in teacher education and in a Vygotskian approach to mentoring (see Elliott 1995). Further investigation is needed by other teacher educators with other cohorts and in other contexts (e.g., inner-city public schools, private schools, charter schools). I will continue to carefully examine if our preservice teachers have had a holistic process of learning to teach that includes sociocultural experiences.

❖ Chapter 8

Vygotsky for Teachers

Outside the Given Realm

Teach by example. That's my motto. I believe that preservice teachers can learn through teaching and researching in collaboration with others. I believe that teacher educators can also learn from these activities. Many teacher educators teach about the wholeness and interconnections of knowledge, but they are missing part of that knowledge base themselves if they work only from their own discipline. Our capacity to learn from each other's viewpoints and to use our newfound multiple perspectives to improve practice can be integrated into our scholarly work. Collaboration can nurture reflection and enrich professional development. I owe much to my colleagues outside the discipline of teacher education. Davydov (1995) reminds me of this when he explains the components of Vygotsky's cultural-historical theory: "The assimilation by a person of historical values of material and spiritual culture in the process of that person's teaching and upbringing takes place through that person's carrying out of personal activity in collaboration with other people" (15). Learning with, and from, each other can provide a validation of change as well as emotional and cognitive support (Osterman and Kottkamp 1993).

The hub of my work has been similar to what John-Steiner (2000) calls interdisciplinary "thought communities." I know there are many other teacher educators working together to reform teacher education (e.g., Rios, McDaniel, and Stowell 1998). I am certainly not single-handedly designing interdisciplinary curricula, although most schooling contexts do not easily support it. Teachers often see themselves as rugged individuals in a profession that breeds more competitiveness than collaboration. Some believe the myth that teachers are supposed to know it all and be autonomous. But Short and Burke (1989) contend that teacher educators need to live their own models. Goodlad (1990) insists that teacher education programs should "be characterized in all respects by the conditions for learning that future teachers are to establish in their own schools and classrooms" (59). Do preservice teachers have the chance to see and experience models of peer collaboration?

There are calls for active partnerships between teacher educators and arts and science faculty who teach subject content to preservice teachers (see Grosso de León 2001). Some teacher educators are beginning to recognize that they can't teach without real school contexts and classroom teachers; what Henson, Koivu-Rybicki, Madigan, and Muchmore (2000) call "outside researchers." They acknowledge that their students are more motivated when they see how everything is connected.

My interdisciplinary work with others has moved me closer to the Vygotskian principles I profess. By working with others, I am attempting to shift the normative structure of teacher preparation in which preservice teachers have limited opportunities to explore interdisciplinary relationships. As John-Steiner (1989, 2000) notes in the context of her Vygotskian interpretation of creativity, insights are gained from exposure to a variety of fields that integrate ideas from multiple perspectives. This notion of multiple perspectives, or the ability to see problems from a variety of points of view, is after all the cornerstone of CUA's conceptual framework. Like my students, I thrive in a collegial atmosphere. I have sought out, embraced, and taught with a community of fine scholars at CUA, at other universities, and abroad because I see teaching as a public, not a private, act. As I have crossed the comfortable boundaries and familiarity of my discipline, I have been able to develop professionally and to share the value of interdisciplinary work with my students. At the university and abroad, I strive to share my passion for interdisciplinary teaching with others as I continue to explore collaborative projects based in sociocultural theory.

I transcended traditional boundaries in my work with a kindergarten teacher and a movement specialist to teach children and preservice teachers through movement education at our campus childcare center (Samaras, Straits, and Patrick 1998). I then asked the preservice teachers to incorporate movement concepts in their units. Sue Straits (who taught the Methods of Physical Education and Health course) and I began discussing how preservice teachers could teach social studies and science concepts more effectively through movement activities. They could integrate those experiences in one interdisciplinary unit instead of submitting two separate units for our courses.

At the time, I was also working with Suzanne Patrick, an early childhood master's student, in an independent study of her yearlong curriculum unit. She was also the kindergarten teacher at the university childcare center. We discussed how Sue could help her integrate movement activities into her unit on the seasons and how her kindergartners would learn with our students. In the situated activity of working with children at our campus athletic center, preservice teachers and young children learned movement interchanges with support from professors in this bodies-on experience.

Sue projected images of leaves, paper snowflakes, or a spring flower on a large wall while children danced out a new understanding of the concepts of cycles, change, and continuity in a unit on the seasons. The visual senses were activated while they were moving their bodies. All of us took part in the dancing. Some preservice teachers giggled, and when one preservice teacher exclaimed she couldn't see how dancing like a leaf was going to make her a better teacher, we talked about how children can use their bodies to internalize physical shapes as well as to explore and express the inner self.

The shared activity among teachers and between preservice teachers and young children enhanced preservice teachers' use of movement in their interdisciplinary units. For example, using the concepts of awareness and beauty in a unit on the oceans, they created dance stories using action terms such as "smooth" or "gliding forward." They mimicked the powerful opening and closing of the body based on the octopus's application of hydraulics and the advancing and retreating tactical strategies of the Maryland crab.

A second example of transcending traditional boundaries involved my collaboration on a major science project funded through the National Science Foundation (see Samaras, Howard, and Wende 2000). Considering the need for interdisciplinary study at the university and recognizing elementary school teachers' need for improved science content knowledge, I teamed with biology faculty in the planning and evaluating of Adventures in Science, an environmental theme-based pilot science program to improve the scientific literacy of non-science majors. I learned a great deal as I worked with Barbara Howard, a clinical biologist and the principal investigator of the grant; Carolee Wende, a microbiologist; and Diane Haddick, a research librarian.

The project involved three sequential courses, and faculty were invited from many disciplines to teach in the courses. I was able to work closely with scientists, geologists, and engineers; I found out how they think and observed their problem-solving strategies. The courses were based on a combination of science disciplines such as biology, chemistry, ecology, engineering, geology, mathematics, meteorology, and physics. Each course included students' collaborative research projects with an emphasis on how scientists work with others to solve social problems and to try to affect public policy. We tried to encourage a population of non-science majors to become excited about the connections within science through hands-on experiences.

My involvement with the grant allowed me to meet and work with preservice teachers during their freshmen and sophomore years when they were required to complete the environmental courses. In their junior year, they took my courses, where I observed a greater appreciation for and application of science content in lessons and research than I had witnessed in former cohorts. For example, in Gabriella's research paper on developing metacognitive skills in young children, she offered the example of teaching her students about why leaves change color:

> Then we started to talk about trees, which led to the question of the importance of trees. They were able to inductively reason why we need trees and the environmental concerns connected to it. It was absolutely exciting.

Amelia took her students outdoors to complete leaf rubbings, leaf presses, and leaf painting as they study the characteristics of leaves. She stated in her lesson objectives, "I feel that it is important for everyone to learn about their environment."

Each course also included numerous field trips and laboratory experiences. Students had an opportunity to collect soil and water samples from nearby rivers, feel the forceful nor'easter on the shores of the Atlantic, and paddle in a canoe on the Anacostia River.

Undergraduate students from many disciplines and with variable levels of science content knowledge worked together to simulate the Conference of the Parties-3 (COP-3), sponsored by the United Nations Framework Convention of Climate Change (UNFCC) in Kyoto, Japan. In Kyoto Redoux, a class reenactment of a United Nations conference, students investigated the positions of many countries on the issue of limiting the emissions of greenhouse gases. Through a series of planning sessions, dialogue, and interaction with peers and faculty from the sciences, education, drama, political science, engineering, and economics disciplines, students gained multiple perspectives on environmental issues in scientific research groups. This learning project involved collective cognition in a group investigation with the support of peers and professors.

In this project, students of many ability levels worked to promote group success toward a mutual goal. They were challenged by real science problems, and the simulation allowed them to submit ideas for group consideration, build upon each other's ideas, and reach a consensus for group action. There were multiple and overlapping student and faculty ZPDs. Students and faculty brought their expertise to the group projects from their respective disciplines. Students worked with professors from various disciplines who supported the Kyoto conference reenactment in this major university community project.

We conducted an evaluation of the process using nontraditional evaluation tools, including portfolios, focus groups, and faculty, team, and self-evaluations to assess perspectives on the Kyoto Redoux project from early childhood and elementary preservice teachers and other non-science majors. The simulation exercise allowed students to feel as if they actually participated in the conference. A politics major stated: "I wanted to let the audience know and believe that I was an actual representative from Japan...I next found myself thinking like I was really from the Japanese coalition." Students learned about environmental science issues, made connections across the sciences and disciplines, collaborated, and cooperated to plan a successful group presentation. The study led us to a better understanding of practical ways to teach science content to non-science majors. It also presented us with a pedagogy that encouraged students to see the relevance of science to their disciplines. We also learned about techniques that promoted problem-solving skills in collaborative contexts and how to better structure and assess students' environmental course experiences.

In each of these learning experiences, I tried to serve as a role model, demonstrating by example that learning to teach is a process that is enriched by interdisciplinary connections. I view teaching as an artistic and analytic endeavor and approach it as a work in progress that has improved through my work with faculty from other disciplines.

Drama Beyond the Theatre

Since 1999, I have been teaching an interdisciplinary course that I co-designed and co-teach with Roland Reed, a drama professor at CUA. We call this ongoing interdisciplinary work Drama Beyond the Theatre, and we have collected data over three years about the experiences of the students who take our class. We are two professors from two different worlds. Roland is a drama professor, a playwright, and a director. I am an education professor, a self-study teacher educator, and a director of teacher education—a different kind of artist than Roland. Yet, we were drawn to a collaborative endeavor to study the relative place and meaning of drama, to learn how to integrate it with other disciplines, and to see how students could apply it to their careers. We eagerly accepted the unpredictable nature of our work and adventure. Embarking on this journey meant that we, like our students, were crossing discipline boundaries with no markers or certainties.

This has been one of my most incredible professional development experiences. I am learning the associations between the Vygotskian approach that I use teaching teachers (Samaras 1998) and a Stanislavskian (1989) method that I learned from Roland. I later discovered that Vygotsky borrowed some of Stanislavsky's drama-coaching techniques in his own work (Kozulin 1999). Roland and I had both worked with children's creative drama, using oral histories, dance exercises, and puppetry, but we had a limited view of how they could be integrated outside our own work. I think of this work as Vygotsky beyond the teacher education classroom and drama beyond the theatre.

Statement of the Problem

There is much research to support the idea that the connections between the arts and academic achievement are very real; integrating the arts into pedagogy enhances the ability to reason, think creatively, and solve problems. These skills transfer to the workplace as students enter adulthood (Caine and Caine 1994; Getty Education Institute for the Arts 1996; Wright 1997). In urban and high-poverty settings, the arts have a significant impact on student improvement in reading and mathematics (Catterall, Chapleau, and Iwanaga 1999). While there have been national initiatives to make the arts part of a core curriculum in schools (Consortium of National Arts Education Associations 1994; Eisner 1998; U. S. Department of Education 1994), these initiatives have had little impact at the university level. College-level students typically complete their art requirement in a non-integrated fashion. This is particularly ineffective for preservice teachers, who may receive little experience with or modeling of arts integration in their own schooling.

Preservice teachers can learn about themselves and human diversity through the arts, yet they are typically given little information about how to use the arts in their teaching. As teachers, they will soon have the opportunity to develop future artists and instill arts appreciation across the curriculum. For example, a teacher training model in England includes drama in education by using the theatre to help students learn about themselves, encourage students to develop empathy for others, teach principles of conflict resolution, and discuss ways to improve racial relations (Catterall, Chapleau, and Iwanaga 1999). Faculty from fine arts and performing arts normally do not view teaching preservice teachers as part of their responsibility. They also know little about self-study practices. Education faculty, excluding arts educators, are normally not knowledgeable about arts instruction and consequently often perpetuate its near-absence in the curriculum.

Roland and I wanted to develop an interdisciplinary course at CUA that enabled students to experience the power of interdisciplinary work and ways to use it to achieve their career goals. I was particularly interested in how preservice teachers could use drama in their pedagogy. Our major course objective is for students to use drama as a conduit for perspective-taking, or taking the perspective of someone other than themselves. Through drama, we are able to teach about conflict resolution and issues relevant to cultural diversity. Perspective-taking exercises enable students to experience abstract principles such as the life and dignity of the human person and the rights of workers. We emphasize our commitment to social justice and moral reasoning by asking students to improvise solutions to human problems and discuss the dilemmas inherent in personal points of view. We believe that knowing our commonalities as humans will move us toward reconciliation and peace, both inner peace and world peace. At the least, we want our students to learn about using drama as a tool and to enjoy it.

Students from all disciplines and majors are invited to practice the tools of drama. They research and adapt acting techniques, exercises, improvisations, and theatre games in a variety of settings and disciplines, such as teaching, counseling, social work, and business. Course activities include introducing students to concepts and practices of drama (especially acting, coaching, and directing, which may be adapted for other uses than the performance of plays, such as formal and informal teaching situations involving children and adults); counseling for educational, psychological, and social services purposes; and working with children in the home.

The time was propitious at our university to be thinking of such a course. A special college task force had been assigned to study interdisciplinary teaching for a new undergraduate college at the university. The task force released a report that validated and supported our thinking. It called for a better grounding in the liberal arts through integration of courses across disciplines, new cross-disciplinary courses, and the broadening of faculty members' perspectives in preparing courses outside their area of specialization. In 1997, the task force noted in their report that *Ex Corde Ecclesiae* encourages faculty to engage in efforts that foster the whole development of the person through the integration of knowledge. Our course proposal was well received by the university and our departments.

During the summer of 1999, the dean supported our teaching efforts abroad as we implemented our drama work with refugees, orphans, and caregivers in Bosnia and Croatia. As we gave service, we also modeled how professors, like students, need to be willing to solve unfamiliar problems and bring their theories into the real world. We tested drama exercises for promoting peace, often in a nonverbal fashion, and returned to teach our course again with new pedagogical and human insights.

Theoretical Framework

In our course, students explore ways to empathize and understand better what it is like to be in someone else's world or on someone else's path. It's a learn-by-doing course, or, using Bruner's (1966) term, enactive representation. It's a course where students use their bodies to learn. Their expressions of what they are learning become iconic when we ask them to create images in their minds and symbolic when they use language to symbolize their experiences (see Wagner 1998).

Through drama exercises, we press students to come to understand the self through others or, in Vygotskian ([1960] 1981) terms, to move from intrapersonal to interpersonal knowledge. We believe that drama moves our students (some more than others) toward higher development through its interactive and perspective-taking work across the overlapping zones of their proximal development. The Vygotskian approach of social interaction and verbalization of ideas affects the cognitive development and cognitive restructuring that lead toward self-knowledge. Language helps students classify, interpret, and make sense of new and ongoing experiences in ways they can't do alone. It serves several purposes: They learn by retelling their stories to others, it provides a platform for peer and professors' scaffolding, it offers redirection, and it facilitates bonding within the class. We also use nonverbal exercises, such as Mirrors, which create a need to pay attention to the actions of others in a silent communion of give and take. The drama activities require students to use their bodies and language to communicate their intentions and feelings; this cultivates a sense of community, care, trust, and respect that we hope students will promote in their own career settings.

Vygotsky was intrigued by Stanislavsky's instruction in the ambiguity of the relationship between the surface utterance and the underlying thought and integrated it in his theory of thought and language (Kozulin 1999). Using the Stanislavsky method, we coach our students in the motivation and intent of the words they enact and often remind them, "Show, don't tell us." We concentrate on mediating the higher psychological processes of memory and imagination to cultivate empathy (Greene 1995; Vygotsky [1960] 1981). We ask students to objectively see the details of the actions of particular human beings and to avoid seeing humans "in general." Using the work of Boal (1992), we stress how humans, unlike animals, are "capable of seeing themselves in the act of seeing, of thinking their emotions, of being moved by their thoughts. They can see themselves here and imagine themselves there; they can see themselves today and imagine themselves tomorrow" (Preface 26).

Methods of Self-Study

We were curious to find out if our course mattered to anyone and how it mattered. Researching students' perceptions of what they learned has been an invaluable evaluation tool. It has allowed us to be responsive to students' needs and to reshape our course each year. What was the impact of our work on students' learning? Did class experiences provoke students to change their angle of vision? We also wanted to find out more about ourselves as educators by examining our own practice through collaborative inquiry—framing and reframing our thinking about teaching through individual and joint exploration and reflection. We raised our own guiding research questions and then collected, analyzed, and presented our data to others to improve our teaching.

- What are our students' perceptions of using drama exercises to learn about themselves and others; that is, to promote perspective-taking?
- What are our perceptions of this interdisciplinary work? Is it valuable to students' and professors' lives, careers, and professional development?
- How might drama be used as a tool for student's knowledge of self; for example, for their self-study?
- Is integrating drama with other disciplines feasible and worthwhile for students and professors?

Participants

Students from many disciplines and backgrounds have taken our course. Enrollment is limited to 16 students to provide the intense and supportive environment required in drama exercises. In the spring 1999 cohort, there were 13 students: 11 undergraduates and 2 graduate students. Twelve females and 1 male enrolled in our course. Two students were majoring in early childhood education, 4 in elementary education, 4 in education studies, and 1 in Latin/secondary education. One student was majoring in anthropology and 1 in psychology. In addition to the 13 students, a graduate student in biomedical engineering and a professor of nursing asked us if they could audit our course, and we agreed.

In the spring 2000 cohort, there were 11 students: 10 undergraduates, and 1 graduate student. All were females. Of those students, 3 were majoring in early childhood education, 2 in elementary education, 4 in education studies, 1 in psychology, and 1 in educational psychology.

The spring 2001 cohort consisted of 16 students: 13 undergraduates and 3 graduate students. Thirteen females and 3 males were enrolled in the course. One student was majoring in early childhood education, 3 in elementary education, 3 in education studies, and 2 in English/secondary education. One student was majoring in marketing and industrial relations, and another was majoring in theological studies. One student majored in communication/media studies, 1 in psychology, 1 in drama, and 2 in musical theatre. There was a waiting list for the spring 2001 semester.

Data Sources

As reflective practitioners, we were the principal instruments for mediating data in our qualitative research (see Taylor 1996). We cooperatively planned, team-taught, and then reflected upon each class session. Through daily communication (e-mail, phone, fax, and face-to-face dialogue), we studied our efforts throughout the semester. In a logbook, I wrote our artistic sketches and reflections and the things that seemed to inspire us. I recorded our notes, students' reactions to class activities, and their post-enactment reflections in an effort to make sense of the thirteen weekly class experiences each semester. Students' projects, assignments, and electronically sent reflections of coursework were collected and copied. We solicited student feedback frequently. Samples of students' final projects were videotaped. University course evaluations were also completed at the end of each semester. We each kept logbooks of our drama work in the Balkans and reflected often on what we were learning.

Data Analysis

We had no preconceived hypotheses and did not subscribe to a simplistic cause-and-effect view of the human experiences that occurred in this artful work. The logbooks and diaries recorded the evolving and shifting relationships that grew out of the drama experiences between us and our students, and among students. Multiple data sources were used to inform this self-study. First, we examined primary data sources, which included professional logs, students' assignments with self-evaluations, written final project presentations, and course evaluations.

Next, we analyzed secondary data sources: field notes and all electronic correspondence. We read and reread our data and made comments in the margins when we saw recurring themes. We used the constant-comparative method (Glaser and Strauss 1967) and theory that we elaborated on and modified as more data became available. We constructed categories; in this case, conceptual elements of students' and professors' thoughts. We noted properties, or conceptual aspects of each category, that emerged from the data. Students' perceptions were coded and then categorized as (1) career connections; (2) finding our humanity; and (3) knowledge of self and others. Professors' perceptions were coded and then categorized as (1) frames for teaching and (2) professional and personal growth.

Findings: Students' Perceptions

Career Connections. Students noted that the course was most worthwhile in terms of its utility for their career goals. A female engineering graduate student devised a skit that debunked stereotypes of female scientists. A psychology major designed a project to use drama in therapy to facilitate the healing of sexually abused children. She shares:

> I know that I will eventually get to the point where this project and this type of therapy will be understood more clearly to me. The fact that I was able to do a project like this during my undergraduate career is great and I know that it has opened up some doorways in my mind—doorways that I will be stepping through next fall in a graduate psychology program.

An educational psychology doctoral candidate who also works as a university practicum liaison asked preservice teachers to role-play the perspective of a parent in a parent-teacher conference. A student who was interested in pursuing a career in counseling found that using a problem card improvisation technique is a great tool for working with teenage unwed moms. Another designed point-of-view scenarios to coach teachers in their work with students whose first language is not English (see Sternberg 1998 for drama activities).

Preservice teachers designed curriculum units incorporating improvisation to explore teaching about disabilities, intergenerational conversations, conflict resolution, teaching reading, examining points of view in Shakespeare plays, developing social skills, democratic classrooms, and character education. I discovered from student teacher supervisors that some were using drama in their teaching. Student comments tell how the drama exercises have moved them to seeing their students' perspectives better. A preservice teacher remarked:

> After I observed all of the projects in class yesterday, I realized that many projects focus on the notion of taking on the role of others. I immediately came to the conclusion that I have been taking on the role of others through studying to become a teacher. Now I realize how important it was for us to do this perspective-taking during our education methods studies.

In a reflection of her final project, a preservice teacher states, "I feel that my activity was able to touch all types of learners. I discovered that drama could be used for educational purposes, which is something I never knew before."

Finding Our Humanity. When students observed and then improvised a street person or when they enacted an oral history interview or when they read a poem in the voice of a character or when they told a favorite story about values, we began to know a part of each other's pasts. The exercises allowed us to recognize that we can understand others on the inside even if on the outside they seem very different from us. Students spoke of the similarities they found between themselves and street people they observed. They noted similarities such as "getting through the day, survival, trying to hold on to our human dignity, and tuning out the world around you if the world around you tunes you out." A student observed a man who appeared to be homeless. He rocked back and forth and sang about how Jesus loves him. After she enacted his actions, she wrote:

> While singing, I didn't feel foolish like I thought I would. Instead, I imagined that no one else was in the room with me and I really concentrated on being happy and joyous. When I was asking [fellow classmates] if they loved Jesus, I felt hurt like my character. The blank faces and faces of confusion were expressed to me through the class reactions, so I understood his feelings more because I was treated in the same manner to a certain degree. This was a great experience. It really challenged me to walk in someone else's moccasins, to feel another's emotions and feelings.

In improvisation exercises, students spoke of sadness, empathy, being judged unfairly, awkwardness, and loneliness. In post-enactment reflections, many expressed gratefulness for their own fortunes and a deeper understanding of human frailties and fragility. We talked about the difference between sympathy and empathy after the case study enactments. A student remarked:

> During the class performance, I really tried to capture what I thought was the nature of my character and the situation in which I saw him. I don't know if the assignment will have a long-lasting effect on me, but I do know that part of my view of the homeless has changed. I know that I need to make sure that I do not allow my sympathy to overtake me and turn into a pity that berates or degrades [people] from the status of the human beings they really are.

In the spring semester 2001, we added the assignment of an empathy poem, or a reading in the voice of someone who is very different from them. For example, one read in the voice of a pedophile, another in the voice of a bigot, and another in the voice of a neurotic. Wow! The readings were a fantastic way for students to recognize how as humans we want to be understood and loved. During the same week we assigned the empathy poems, I was rereading van Manen's (1977) article on linking ways of knowing. Each year, we place the article on the library reserve file for our preservice teachers to read. I know most students have difficulty understanding it, yet it is one of the major research studies that was used to develop our reflective teacher model over a decade ago. In explaining the works of Dilthey ([1914] 1962), van Manen (1977) writes:

> Understanding involves the capacity to grasp the inner realities of the human world—empathy. In ordinary English, we speak of an "understanding look" which suggests more than mere objective knowledge. In Dilthey's terms, we understand ourselves and others only in re-experiencing, by inserting our experienced life into every form of expression of our own and others' lives. Understanding is reserved to designate the operation in which the mind grasps the mind of the other person. It is not a purely cognitive operation of the mind at all, but that special moment when life understands life (214).

I realized that I had been trying to teach preservice teachers to understand how to see things from the point of view of the student, of parents, and of society, but I had only taught it as a purely intellectual process. I observed how when they cast themselves into someone else's nature, they embodied it. They were learning dramatic empathy and possibly caring empathy that would help them to know the people they would work with and the students they would teach (Verducci 1998).

Drama character exercises can also help students deal with anxiety before groups as they take on the role of someone else. After one very self-conscious student enacted her case study of someone else, Roland offered his response through electronic mail:

> *Reed Electronic Mail, 14 February 2001*
> I am moved by your reflections and most pleased that you allowed yourself to focus on your character to the extent that you could eliminate most of your "self" consciousness. That is an important step toward true empathy. If you do concentrate on something or someone outside yourself, besides getting rid of self-consciousness, you will find that your fuller attention on the outside focus will be more interesting and more productive. You've gotten off to a wonderful start.

Knowledge of Self and Others. As a mode of learning, students used spectator talk to recount or recreate experiences that were real or imagined. After her interview, a student wrote to us through electronic mail:

> I enjoyed listening to the results of everyone's interviews yesterday. What I found most interesting was that when I read mine, I became convinced of what I was saying. I think there is definitely something to reading something to others. When I read it at home, I understood it and enjoyed it as Butch's experience. When I had to read it to the class, I had to be aware of the fact that I was communicating. I needed to be heard and understood. This was like Butch, or anyone else, telling a story. He spoke with the intention of being understood. My desire for the class to understand took me through the motions of storytelling, as if it were my own story. You both are right. I think this exercise taught us more about each other than the people we interviewed. I think I learned a lot about my classmates.

Our students also used participant talk to explore, theorize, gather information, and solve problems. For example:

> I appreciated the comments I received from the class the most. I had many misconceptions about why my project would work best with inner dialogue. During my dress rehearsal [a project preview sketch], the class challenged those ideas and strengthened the discussion segment of my project immensely.

After improvisations students described how they came to know new things about themselves; for example, "I learned that I try to avoid conflict" and "I think I have more positive feelings toward the homeless than the soup-kitchen women."

Students reflected on how they came to know a side of their families they never knew before through oral history interviews with a family member. Many pointed out how they could now see a part of themselves in their mothers and sisters. After enacting an interview with her mother, a student announced to the class, "Adults really [are] little kids too." A student became very interested in her father's escape from a war-torn country and stated, "He doesn't see his story as interesting; [he] only [sees it] as a negative story that makes him look bad, even though he is the hero in it." One student brought us closer to her mother's struggle. She wrote: "Thinking back on the interview with my mother, I know that being a teenage mother was a difficult, difficult thing for my mother. It makes me proud every time I think of her story." Another reflected in her oral history assignment:

> Realizing what my mother's life was like reveals the reasons why she acts in
> certain ways around people and also kind of tells why she raised my brothers and
> sisters and myself the way she did. I think I understand a little more about where
> my mom came from and what important things meant to her as a little girl.

A student who described her own birth through her mother's eyes
explained, "I was able to feel what my mom's emotions were in a way I
don't think I had ever experienced." A semester after she completed our
course, her mother died of cancer. I cried and remembered her mother's
story. When students dramatized their oral history family interviews,
they shared a part of their pasts with us. In a sense, the drama immortal-
ized their family member in our memories.

Another new assignment that we added in spring 2001 was to ask
students to read a revelation poem, or a poem that reveals something
about them that is usually hidden. The poem enables them to do many
things. It is a way for them to tell us something about themselves that
they don't want us to miss. Reading the poem may be easier than telling
the class, or the poem may be the only way they can say it. The poem
readings allow us to hear each other as we begin to trust and bond. One
student read from a book of writings for the teenage soul. She read about
finding the gray, whereas before she only saw black and white. She
struggles to reconstruct her dualistic world outlook. This helped me to
know more about this education student. After class, I commented
privately to her how I enjoyed her reading. She smiled and our eyes told
us we both understood. I'm so glad for her revelation!

Findings: Professors' Perceptions

Frames for Teaching. Working in concert, Roland and I were able to
draw associations between our fields of study as we brought them to bear
on our problem-solving for this course. For example, despite the
vernacular of our distinct disciplines, we quickly saw the association
between the concepts of scaffolding and side-coaching. Vygotsky
([1960] 1981) claims that:

> Any function in the child's cultural development appears twice, or on two planes.
> First it appears on the social plane, and then on the psychological plane. First it
> appears between people as an interpsychological category, and then within the
> child as an intrapsychological category (163).

Similarly, side-coaching "alters the traditional relationship of teacher-student, creating a moving relation...[and] allows the teacher-director an opportunity to step into the excitement of playing [learning] in the same space, with the same focus, as the players" (Spolin 1999, 28). This technique allows the director (or teacher) to view the overall presentation while seeing what the individual student-actor needs within the group and allows the teacher-director to work on a problem with the student's effort.

Logbook, 1 February 1999

Denise was very concerned about structuring drama for her classroom. I knew that other preservice teachers would need that information as well, since classroom management is always a concern for teachers. I found a chapter in John Needlands' (1985) book on ways of structuring drama and took some notes. When I spoke with Roland about the need for structure in drama, he remarked that drama entailed a "concentration of attention" as discussed by Spolin and Stanislavsky.

Sorting through our different language, I understood how teachers might see classroom structure as keeping students on task by demanding students' attention. In drama, the lure is the action and the attention to the use of imagination. The director side-coaches to help students maintain their focus. Teachers could examine the language they use to keep students on task and focused. Neither classroom learning nor dramatic expression can be imposed. You can't force a student to learn or act, but the coach can help maintain an unbroken focus by preserving an atmosphere of concentration. How interesting. I shared this with the class as well.

We easily discovered other associations; in particular, we discovered that we both focused on teaching about perspective-taking. I taught preservice teachers to view teaching situations from the perspective of students, parents, society, and teacher within our reflective teacher framework. Roland taught drama majors how to apply the Stanislavskian "magic if," or how to put oneself on the plane of make-believe in someone else's situation. Roland came closer to the realities of schools by coaching preservice teachers' curriculum projects while I observed students enacting, and not just talking about, the perspectives of others. This happened best through drama exercises, what Spolin (1999) calls "physicalization," or inner action through exercises that focus attention on "the where" and "the who" of a situation.

Through my trip to Croatia and Roland's numerous trips to Bosnia, we acquired a heightened sense of how to teach conflict resolution and brought it back to our class when we taught our course the following spring. Below is an excerpt from his diary:

Reed Balkan Diary, 26 June 1999
Each day is spent working alternatively with twenty teenagers and with orphanage directors and caregivers from nine other orphanages from various cities and towns in Bosnia and the SOS Kinderhof from Sarajevo. The other Trauma Team members focused on the adults, dealing with anger management, conflict resolution concepts, and the importance of the consistent application and enforcement of rules. I followed up conceptual sessions with improvisations and exercises designed to identify sources of anger, promote cooperative problem- solving, and reverse role-playing to develop a sense of an antagonist's perspective. Anastasia and I had developed many of these ideas and techniques in our spring 99 course at CUA. Between the sessions with caregivers, I worked in similar ways with the teenagers.

The combination of anger, affection, hostility, caring, depression, and exuberance that was constantly exhibited by the group both moved me and exhausted me. Group discussions and improvisations dealing with anger and grievances frequently led to the edge of chaos and back to quiet reflection and considered responses. By the third day, the work and play, while still moderately unruly, had become wholly good-natured and mostly cooperative. "Please come back!" was the most frequently translated response at the end of the last session.

Professional and Personal Growth*.* The openness of our self-study led to a high level of professional and personal growth that could not have happened outside the context of our interdisciplinary work. We cooperated and negotiated easily. A student wrote in her course evaluation, "They worked wonderfully together. They are the yin and the yang of teaching."

I found we were very similar but very different in many ways. Roland uses bold, but indirect, teaching strokes to shake students up and shatter the fences that have kept them from sorting things out for themselves. I try to offer a safe class structure and guidance, although I have also become more of a risk-taker in creating new challenges for students and myself. Roland writes that I offered him new insights into his own field by my "keen ability to make creative connections."

Logbook, 8 February 1999
Roland takes the lead today with his expertise in using and developing voice. We decided this would be good since we observed that many of

our students needed it. He is very modest about his many talents in drama and doesn't bring attention to himself. I am more demanding for the most part. I get results in a different way than he does, but he doesn't criticize me. He continues to model his humble style. This modeling helps me see how I am not like him. His approach is more indirect and quiet as he refocuses and coaches the class in drama exercises. I ask myself, "How can I do this better?"

We, too, were course participants. I did many of the drama exercises along with students, and Roland worked through the details of curriculum units that integrated drama. When our students read their revelation and empathy poems, we read ours, too. Like our students, I am learning to show, not tell, how I feel. As professors, we both allowed ourselves to be vulnerable to mistakes and open to letting our students know us. For example, Roland read a poem about how his ancestors used their hands to work, while writers like him try to change the world with only a pen in hand. I read a feminist poem about a journey that was difficult to begin but liberating.

Sharing our pedagogical and content knowledge enriched our knowledge and practice in this team-teaching experience. I discovered how to use and assess drama techniques to promote perspective-taking and conflict resolution across many disciplines. Our sharing aloud enabled us to hear each other's thinking and synthesize and alter our misconceptions and mistakes. We held increasingly higher standards for ourselves and for our students and continuously reaffirmed the seriousness and power of using the arts to teach. This work also reaffirmed my thinking about how learning does not have to occur in isolation and is enhanced through collaboration for professors and students alike. Interdisciplinary work can take professors beyond the comfortable boundaries and familiarity of their work while inspiring and renewing a passion for their own discipline. We hope that our work will encourage professors to collaborate in the shared responsibility of preparing teachers. I make a point of promoting our work on campus and presenting each semester's work at national and international professional conferences (Samaras with Reed 2000, 2001a, 2001b).

Roland easily became a contributor to teacher preparation, and I learned much about using drama as I prepared preservice teachers and students from other majors. Our multiple lenses and expertise helped improve and support our teaching, which we recognize as dynamic and always under creation. Through our collaborative efforts, we found that drama can provide a safe, but very real, haven from which to explore a multiplicity of views. The drama exercises catapulted students into fresh perspectives, and suddenly and for a brief and frozen moment, we watched them see things about others, and themselves, that were hidden or not obvious. We discovered that drama could help communicate the need for and value of human diversity while bridging many disciplines and careers. I often looked back and read my journal logs. I began to understand my attraction to this and other collaborative ventures that were elucidated through my self-study. The log below highlights my sense of wonder:

Logbook, 9 January 1999

I am a student again who is new to the power of drama but not to the power of the arts. I insisted that Roland check the topics I had typed for our syllabus. He explained that he knew from our many planning sessions that I already had certain things in mind and that he would support that teaching of content through the mechanics of the theatre. I was beginning to understand this scaffold he was staging for me. I had been dancing around the arts, notions of feminism, and the connections between the cognitive and the emotive realms.

I looked back, and it suddenly all made sense. I enrolled in a modern dance class I hadn't taken for about fifteen years. I lay on the floor with my arms stretched out to each side and melted into the floor as the teacher asked us to find our center and to feel the imprint of our spine in the imaginary sand. I was home and free again.

❖ Chapter 9

Implications: So What?

As I reflect on the whole of who I am, I can understand this place where I have temporarily arrived. Yet I know the journey will continue, especially in my interdisciplinary work. That I arrived at this place was no coincidence. There was the lure toward perspective-taking in the CUA reflective teacher framework and in my drama work. I found the threads of why nurturance was a central concept in my teaching as I attempted to know my students better through professional assignments that tapped into the personal. My searching for ways for students to share their God-given gifts with each other in mentoring relationships and for me to do the same all seemed to fit with who I was and what I did. I believed that individuals learned best in structured support systems that helped them practice theory in actual settings because I had lived that model in my own life. I was always moving toward the big picture in my interdisciplinary work as I provided opportunities for students to conduct their work in wider circles. Practicing collaboration with individual responsibility was what I came to know and live. A community is the sum of its parts. If the development of those individual parts is full, the result will lead to what is good for the whole. The essential lessons I learned from my life experiences have now come full circle in my teaching.

Early lessons influenced the ways I have come to know students because of my belief in the social and cultural influences that have shaped their development. Throughout the book, I have given testimony to the social and historical forces that have shaped my development and teaching that I discovered through the self-study of my teaching practices. In this reframing of self, I have come to understand why I was attracted to Vygotskian principles as I prepare teachers in my education methods courses and in my interdisciplinary work with others. While I practiced Vygotskian principles in my own teaching, I slowly learned to recognize my own practical theory, which has grown richer over time and which, in turn, I offer to my students.

In my efforts to reshape how I teach teachers, I now see Vygotsky as my revolutionary companion. While constructing this Vygotskian connection, I discovered many others whom I could identify along the way: Bob Bullough (1994a), Gary Knowles and Ardra Cole (with C. S. Presswood 1994), William Pinar and Madeleine Grumet (1976), Grumet (1988), Kathleen Weiler (1988), Mary Catherine Bateson (1990), Penelope Peterson (1997), and Vera John-Steiner (1985). When I read Belenky, Clinchy, Goldberger, and Tarule (1986), I thought about where authority lay in my own decisions. Similarly, when I read Grumet's (1981) reconstruction of educational experience, I thought more about how my present situation influenced my understanding of the past. As I looked deeply inside myself and acknowledged the realities, the histories, and the social structures that shaped my teaching, I thought about my interpretations, choices, and commitments as an active agent in my own learning and teaching. Through my own autobiographical narrative, I came to understand how my schooling had distorted and shaped my perceptual lens and how what I learned there might impact my future.

In this book, I have also emphasized that preservice teachers deserve firsthand experience in a Vygotskian approach in their own learning to fully appreciate or comprehend the ramifications and implications of theory to their teaching practice. I have offered my ways of knowing students, situating learning, structuring social mediation, and working within learning ZPDs.

I made these connections slowly and typically with childlike surprise. It took some time before I could see the patterns of feminism and self-determination in my teaching. I believe that if we look hard enough, things that are right in front of us will allow us to know ourselves and the gifts we can give to the world. At any rate, I am enjoying this process, despite its difficult and ambiguous nature. In my quest for an authenticity of self in my teaching, I will no doubt unearth other jewels if only I keep looking. I guess that's the real point, isn't it? The asking and especially the searching that have led me to a broader view.

I suggest that new types of learning can help preservice teachers cope with the situations they will confront in their classrooms: the newness of the context, the sometimes urgent need to solve problems, the many different versions of humanity they will encounter among their students and colleagues. I believe that we must create a climate of collaboration in which courageous teaching can be cultivated and for which students can take ownership for their learning. We must be both patient and ambitious about processes that will slowly change the very culture of the school and the climate for learning. Teachers can create wonderful new compositions for learning when they create professional communities for themselves. They must have professional time and workspace to plan within and across grade levels and subjects and assess students' learning and opportunities to learn from each other. Their learning will build, like students' learning, over time. Teachers can be proactive in making and not just receiving curriculum changes. Teachers can be the change agents in schools, counties, and states when they take first steps in unknown waters that will chart the way for others. I summarize some of what I came to understand about the role of teacher educators through a self-study of my teaching practices.

Teacher educators can:

- provide opportunities to recognize one's own teaching perspective and those of others
- strive to know the culture of preservice teachers using relational teaching
- encourage risk-taking in a supportive environment
- maintain a climate of high expectations for preservice teachers as they learn, but with sensitivity to the learner's understanding and development
- situate the technical components of teaching within conceptual frames of teaching; for example, teach how to do short- and long-range planning or how to align classroom management with personal theory
- structure learning opportunities for problem-based and interdisciplinary learning with and through others; for example, interpersonal and intrapersonal knowledge using dialogue as the central medium for learning, reflecting, and personal theory-building
- target and support preservice teachers within their ZPDs, or bandwidths of competence, to enable them to grow by working with more capable others; for example, cooperating teachers and peers
- promote shared knowledge; that is, collective cognitive formats or multiple opportunities to form a relationship with an audience (e.g., in dyads, small groups, cohorts, seminars) to promote cognitive, affective, and collegial support
- design field experiences that situate coursework and promote exposure to the social, motivational, and curricular dilemmas inherent in teaching
- relate field experiences to earlier coursework in childhood development and educational psychology
- require continuous self-study, self-evaluation, and peer assessment
- model a sociocultural approach of teaching so preservice teachers can experience a model they might use in their own teaching
- create awareness of institutionalized school cultures and their subgroup cultures

- involve preservice teachers in school-family programs
- facilitate reflection of cultural, historical, and political influences on teaching and testing
- utilize and appreciate the arts as a teaching tool
- model intrinsic and lifelong learning
- craft and practice interdisciplinary teaching teams
- work with cooperating teachers on school and university goals
- promote a shared responsibility for teacher preparation with content specialists

With others, I have researched the role of the cooperating teacher as scaffolders. Exemplary scaffolders monitor, facilitate, and contribute to preservice teachers' understanding of teaching tools. Our preservice teachers were most successful in implementing a unit when the cooperating teacher provided structure while allowing them freedom and the opportunity to claim ownership of their learning and teaching.

Cooperating teachers can:

- build upon preservice teachers' culture and strengths
- allow for graded and incremental teaching responsibility, with support geared to each student's current level; that is, provide guided assistance within the preservice teacher's ZPD
- maintain a climate of high expectations
- dialogue about short-range and long-range planning or placing the immediate within the bigger picture—regularly and frequently
- insist on mutual planning time and encourage preservice teachers to take the initiative in teaching responsibilities
- promote self-regulated learning through supportive engagement
- provide opportunities for preservice teachers to discuss their course learning and personal theories while they are teaching and reflecting in an actual classroom when problems arise
- break down tasks as needed, with adjustments to the learner's responses work as co-explorer and co-teacher with preservice teachers but also facilitate independent teaching experiences
- share metacognitive analysis of pupil learning and the classroom ethos
- provide constructive context-specific feedback about the teaching of the preservice teacher
- have faith in preservice teachers' abilities and what has yet to be born
- require continuous self-evaluation
- invite the preservice teacher into the school community and teaching profession; for example, help them seek out school resource people and familiarize them with the school and its politics
- provide opportunities for preservice teachers to work with families

One of the greatest gifts I have received from this writing is that it has validated my ownership of my teaching as I acknowledge who I am and what that has to do with my teaching and my students' learning. I invite others to practice self-study and to explore those places for themselves. I offer this writing in the hope that my work will cause others to contemplate the effectiveness of current practices and to adapt what is useful here to their particular contexts. I propose that others examine the support systems that are in place before the student-teaching experience and to consider what opportunities preservice teachers have for examining the self and integrity in their own teaching.

Innovation and learning are lifelong processes that can be modeled through one's own teaching and self-study practices. I am thankful for a teaching life of abundance, enriched by its multiplicity, mutuality, and challenges. I have been blessed by many circles of support and love in my personal and professional life that have provided wonderful opportunities for personal and professional growth. My favorite part of this writing is that I am ever evolving; one's understanding of a role never ends (Sarason 1999; Stanislavsky 1989). I have developed a theoretical frame for my scholarship of self-study, and I go to the edge because I know it's what I need to do rather than accept the status quo. This beginning work on crafting a pedagogy for educational change using Vygotskian principles is an example of that. I have always grown the most when I walked to the edge and into an unknown path that called out to me. Predetermined destinations do not lead us to new roads. See you on the path.

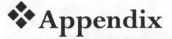 # Appendix

---

CUA Reflective Teacher Model

Preservice Teachers' Reflection of:

Social, Motivational, and Curriculum Dilemmas in Teaching

School Context

Preservice Teacher

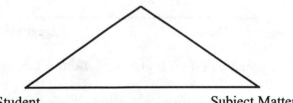

Student   Subject Matter

Reflective Levels

Technical—How to
Interpretive—What is, what it means
Critical—Why, what ought to be

Figure 2.1: CUA Reflective Teacher Model:
A Conceptual Framework for Teacher Education

Samaras Self-Study Model

Teacher Educators' Self-Study of:

Social, Motivational, and Curriculum Dilemmas
in Teaching Preservice Teachers

University/School Context

Teacher Educator

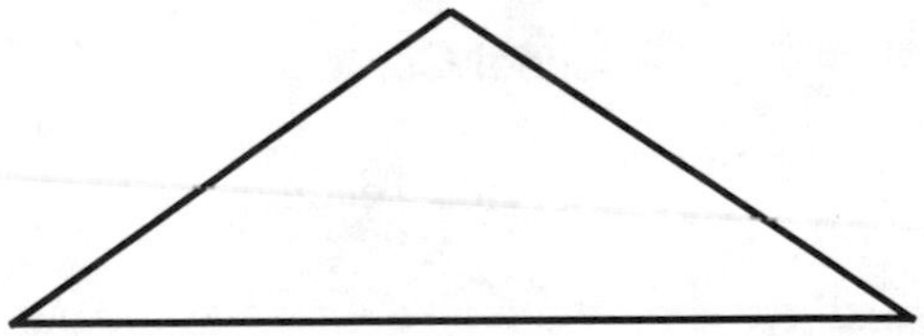

Preservice Teacher   Subject Matter

Vygotskian Principles Using Reflective Levels

Knowing Students—How, What, Why
Situating Learning—How, What, Why
Structuring Social Mediation—How, What, Why
Learning Zones—How, What, Why

Figure 2. 2: Samaras Self-Study Model
(Adapted from CUA Reflective Teacher Model)

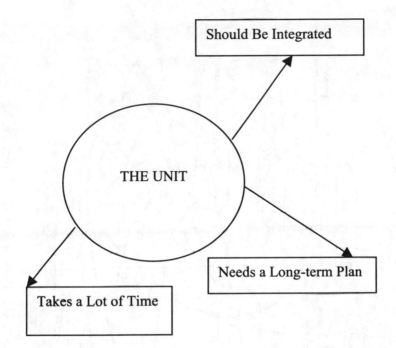

Figure 4.1: Pre-Planning Concept Map of Unit Planning
(Student Project: E. M. Dwan O'Leary 1998)

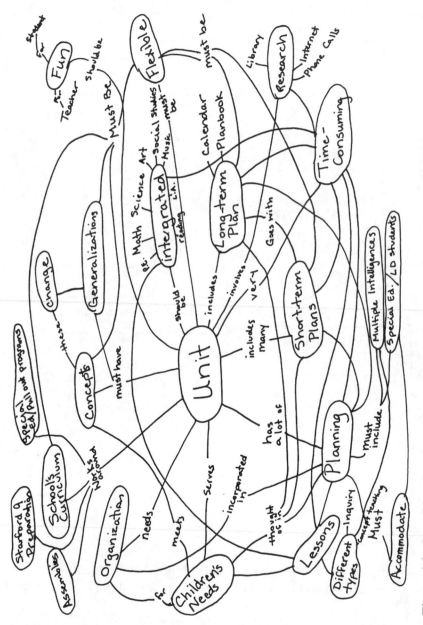

Figure 4.2:   Post-Planning Concept Map of Unit Planning (Student Project: E. M. Dwan O'Leary 1998)

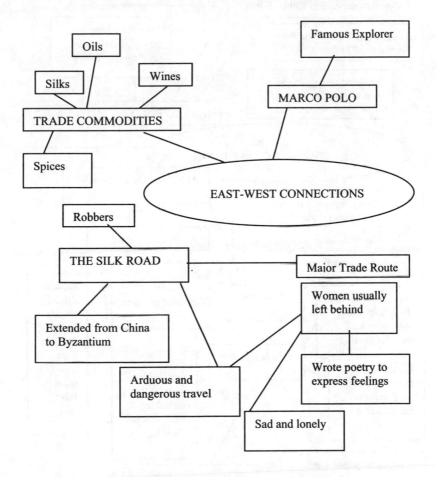

Figure 4.3: Pre-Planning Concept Map of Background Knowledge of East-West Connections (Student Project: A. Walker Korahais 1995)

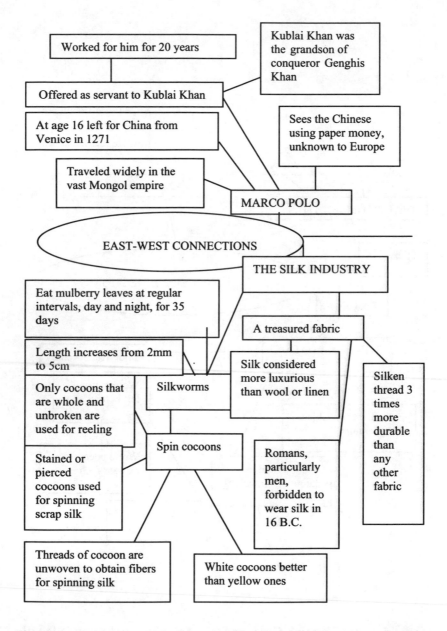

Worked for him for 20 years

Offered as servant to Kublai Khan

Kublai Khan was the grandson of conqueror Genghis Khan

At age 16 left for China from Venice in 1271

Sees the Chinese using paper money, unknown to Europe

Traveled widely in the vast Mongol empire

MARCO POLO

EAST-WEST CONNECTIONS

THE SILK INDUSTRY

Eat mulberry leaves at regular intervals, day and night, for 35 days

A treasured fabric

Length increases from 2mm to 5cm

Silkworms

Silk considered more luxurious than wool or linen

Silken thread 3 times more durable than any other fabric

Only cocoons that are whole and unbroken are used for reeling

Spin cocoons

Stained or pierced cocoons used for spinning scrap silk

Romans, particularly men, forbidden to wear silk in 16 B.C.

Threads of cocoon are unwoven to obtain fibers for spinning silk

White cocoons better than yellow ones

Figure 4.4: Post-Planning Concept Map of Background Knowledge of East-West Connections (Student Project: A. Walker Korahais 1995)

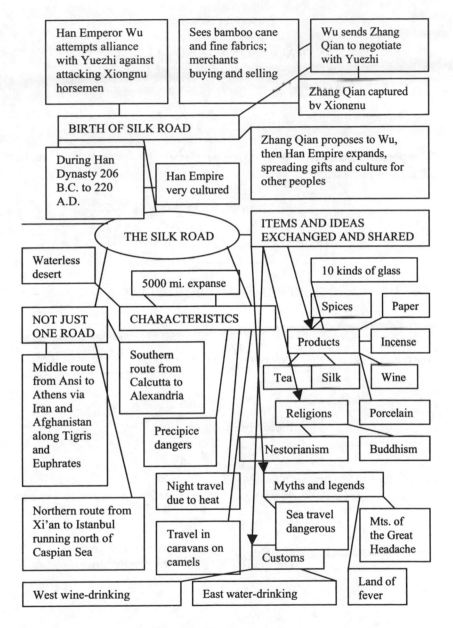

Figure 4.4—Continued.

Anastasia P. Samaras

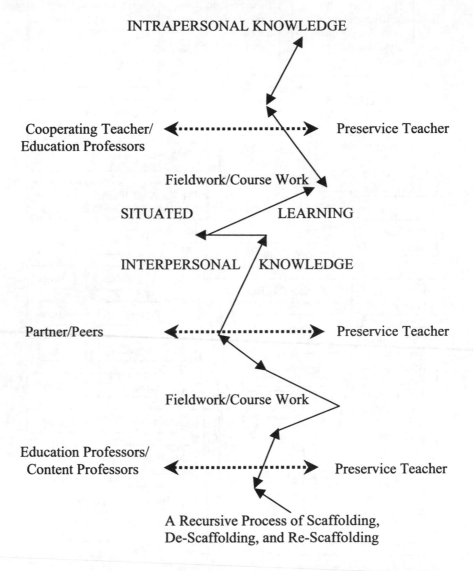

Preservice Teacher

INTRAPERSONAL KNOWLEDGE

Cooperating Teacher/ Preservice Teacher
Education Professors

Fieldwork/Course Work

SITUATED LEARNING

INTERPERSONAL KNOWLEDGE

Partner/Peers Preservice Teacher

Fieldwork/Course Work

Education Professors/ Preservice Teacher
Content Professors

A Recursive Process of Scaffolding,
De-Scaffolding, and Re-Scaffolding

Figure 5.1: Structuring Social Mediation

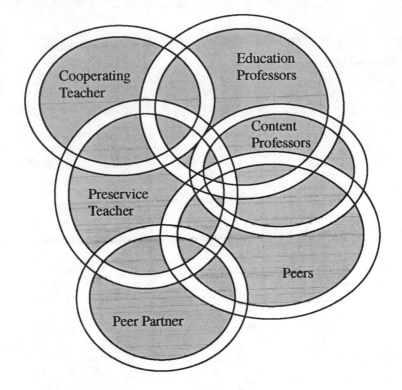

Figure 6.1: Multiple and Overlapping ZPDs
(Adapted from Hansen, Dirckinck-Holmfeld, Lewis and Rugelj 1999)

Pre-active Planning	Interactive Planning	Post-active Planning
Personal Teaching Goals	Mid-term Self-Evaluation	Final Self-Evaluation Exit Interview
Class Goals	Dialogue	Class Debriefing
Pre-Planning Concept Map/ Planning	Teach Unit	Post-Planning Concept Map Planning Paper
Pre-Planning Concept Map/ Content	Research and Teach	Post-Planning Concept Map/ Content
Background Knowledge	Research/Teach Unit	Final Background Knowledge Paper
Author's Chair	Formative Assessment	Final Evaluation of Unit
Lesson Sketches	Feedback from Teacher/Professor	Assessment by Self/Teacher/ Professor
Lesson Plans	Coaching from Peer/Teacher	Reflection on Lesson
Participant Observation	Teach Small/Large Group	Self/Teacher Assessment
Reflective Journals	Ongoing Feedback from Professors	Progress Report Paper
Cooperative Search	Peer Teaching	Peer Review
Field-trip Lesson	Field-trip	Assessment by Self/Professor
Shadow Science Lessons	Teach Science Lessons	Assessment by Self/Professor
Co-Planning with Peers/Teacher	Mid-Evaluation by Teacher	Final Evaluation by Teacher
Co-Plan Unit	Co-Implement Unit	Showcase Portfolio

Figure 6.2: Support Structures in Developing an Interdisciplinary Unit

❖Bibliography

American Association of Colleges for Teacher Education. 1990. *RATE IV. Teaching teachers: Facts and figures.* Washington, D.C.: American Association of Colleges for Teacher Education.

Armaline, W. D., and R. L. Hoover. 1989. Field experience as a vehicle for transformation: Ideology, education, and reflective practice. *Journal of Teacher Education* 40 (2): 42–48.

Aronson, E. 1997. *The jigsaw classroom: Building cooperation in the classroom.* 2nd ed. New York: Longman.

Au, K. H. 1990. Changes in a teacher's views of interactive comprehension instruction. In *Vygotsky and Education: Instructional implications and applications of sociohistorical psychology,* edited by L. C. Moll. New York: Cambridge University Press.

Azmitia, M. 1988. Peer interaction and problem solving: When are two heads better than one? *Child Development* 59: 87–96.

Bakhtin, M. M. 1981. *The dialogic imagination: Four essays by M. M. Bakhtin.* Edited by M. Holquist. Translated by C. Emerson and M. Holquist. Austin: University of Texas Press.

Ball, A. F. 2000. Teachers' developing philosophies on literacy and their use in urban schools: A Vygotskian perspective on internal activity and teacher change. In *Vygotskian perspectives on literacy research: Constructing meaning through collaborative inquiry,* edited by C. D. Lee and P. Smagorinsky. Cambridge, UK: Cambridge University Press.

Bartolome, L. 1994. Beyond the methods fetish. *Harvard Educational Review* 64 (2): 173–194.

Bateson, M. C. 1990. *Composing a life.* New York: Plume.

Belenky, M. F., B. M. Clinchy, N. R. Goldberger, and J. M. Tarule. 1986. *Women's ways of knowing: The development of self, voice, and mind.* New York: Basic Books.

Bendixen-Noe, M. K., and S. S. Redick. 1995. Teacher development theory: A comparison between traditional-aged and nontraditional-aged beginning secondary teachers. *Action in Teacher Education* 37 (1): 52–59.

Berk, L. E., and A. Winsler. 1995. *Scaffolding children's learning: Vygotsky and early childhood education.* Washington, D.C.: National Association for the Education of Young Children.

Berlak, A., and H. Berlak. 1981. *Dilemmas of schooling: Teaching and social change.* London and New York: Methuen.

———. 1987. Teachers working with teachers to transform schools. In *Educating teachers: Changing the nature of pedagogical knowledge,* edited by J. Smyth. Philadelphia: Falmer Press.

Bivens, J. A. 1990. Children's scaffolding children in the classroom: Can this metaphor completely describe the process of group problem solving? Paper presented at the Annual Meeting of the American Educational Research Association, Boston, Mass.

Boal, A. 1992. *Games for actors and non-actors.* Translated by A. Jackson. New York: Routledge.

Bodrova, E., and D. J. Leong. 1996. *Tools of the mind: The Vygotskian approach to early childhood education.* Englewood Cliffs, N.J.: Prentice Hall.

Bogden, R. C., and S. K. Biklen. 1992. *Qualitative research for education: An introduction to theory and methods.* Boston: Allyn and Bacon.

Bower, G. 1992. Emotion and memory. In *Handbook of emotion and memory,* edited by S. A. Christianson. Hillsdale, N.J.: Lawrence Erlbaum.

Bransford, J. D., A. L. Brown, and R. R. Cocking, eds. 1999. *How people learn: Brain, mind, experience, and school.* Committee on Developments in the Science of Learning, Commission on Behavioral and Social Sciences and Education, National Research Council. Washington, D.C.: National Academy Press.

Briggs, K. C., and I. Briggs. Myers. 1991. *Myers-Briggs type indicator.* Palo Alto, Calif.: Consulting Psychologists Press.

Britzman, D. P. 1991. *Practice makes practice: A critical study of learning to teach.* Albany, N.Y.: State University of New York Press.

Brodkey, L. 1996. *Writing permitted in designated areas only.* Minneapolis, Minn.: University of Minnesota Press.

Brown, A. 1994. The advancement of learning. *Educational Researcher* 23 (8): 4–12.

Bruner, J. S. 1966. *Toward a theory of instruction.* Cambridge, Mass.: Harvard University Press.

———. 1985. Vygotsky: A historical and conceptual perspective. In *Culture, communication, and cognition: Vygotskian perspectives,* edited by J. V. Wertsch. New York: Cambridge University Press.

———.1987. Prologue to the English edition. In *The collected works of L. S. Vygotsky,* edited by R. W. Rieber and A. S. Carton. New York: Plenum Press.

Bullough, R. V. 1994a. When more or less is not enough: Rethinking preservice teacher education. Paper presented at the Annual Meeting of the American Educational Research Association, New Orleans, La.

———.1994b. Personal history and teaching metaphors: A self-study of teaching as conversation. *Teacher Education Quarterly* 21 (1): 107–120.

Bullough, R. V., and S. Pinnegar. 2001. Guidelines for quality in autobiographical forms of self-study research. *Educational Researcher* 30 (3): 13–21.

Caine, R. N., and G. Caine. 1994. *Making connections: Teaching and the human brain.* Menlo Park, Calif.: Addison-Wesley.

Campbell, P. F., and G. G. Fein, eds. 1986. *Young children and micro-computers.* Englewood Cliffs, New Jersey: Prentice Hall.

Catterall, J. S., R. Chapleau, and J. Iwanaga. (1999). Involvement in the arts and human development. In *Champions of change: The impact of the arts on learning,* edited by E. B. Fiske. Washington, D.C.: Arts Education Partnership and President's Committee on the Arts and the Humanities.

Cochran-Smith, M. 1991. Learning to teach against the grain. *Harvard Educational Review* 61 (3): 279–310.

Cole, A. L., and J. G. Knowles. 1995. Methods and issues in a life history approach to self-study. In *Teachers who teach teachers: Reflections on teacher education,* edited by T. Russell and F. Korthagen. Bristol, Pa.: Falmer Press.

Cole, M., and S. Scribner. 1978. Introduction. In *Mind in society,* edited and translated by M. Cole, V. John-Steiner, S. Schribner, and E. Souberman. Cambridge, Mass.: Harvard University Press.

Collinson, V. 1999. Redefining teacher excellence. *Theory Into Practice* 38 (1): 4–11.

Collinson, V., M. Killeavy, and H. J. Stephenson. 1999. Exemplary teachers: Practicing an ethic of care in England, Ireland, and the United States. *Journal for a Just and Caring Education* 5 (4): 349–366.

Conway, M. A., and D. A. Beckerian. 1988. Characteristics of vivid memories. In *Practical aspects of memory,* vol. 2, edited by M. M. Gruneberg, P. E. Morris, and R. N. Sykes. New York: John Wiley.

Dalton, S. 1989. *Teachers as assessors and assistors.* Paper presented at the annual meeting of the American Educational Research Association, San Francisco, Calif. ERIC Document Reproduction Service No. ED 313 324.

Darling-Hammond, L. 1997. *The right to learn: A blueprint for creating schools that work.* San Francisco: Jossey-Bass.

Davydov, V. V. 1995. The influence of L. S. Vygotsky on education theory, research, and practice. *Educational Researcher* 24 (3): 12–21.

Dewey, J. 1938. *Experience and education.* New York: Macmillan.

———.[1900] 1990. *The school and society and The child and the curriculum.* Chicago: The University of Chicago Press.

Dillenbourg, P., ed. 1999. *Collaborative learning: Cognitive and computational approaches.* Oxford, UK: Elsevier Science.

Dilthey, W. [1914] 1962. *Pattern and meaning in history.* Edited by Hans P. Rickman. London: Heinemann.

Dixon-Krauss, L. 1996. *Vygotsky in the classroom: Mediated literacy instruction and assessment.* White Plains, N.Y.: Longman Publishers.

Doolittle, P. E. 1995. Vygotsky and the socialization of literacy. *Reading: Exploration and discovery* 16: 45–50.

Edwards, A. 1995. Teacher education: Partnerships in pedagogy? *Teaching and Teacher Education* 11 (6): 595–610.

Eisner, E. W. 1998. *The kinds of schools we need: Personal essays.* Portsmouth, N.H.: Heinemann.

Elbaz, F. 1981. The teacher's "practical knowledge": Report of a case study. *Curriculum Inquiry* 11 (1): 43–71.

El'Konin, D. B. 1968. The problem of instruction and development in the works of L. S. Vygotsky, *Soviet Psychology* 7: 34–41.

Elliott, B. 1995. Developing relationships: significant episodes in professional development. *Teachers and Teaching: Theory and Practice* 1 (2): 247–264.

Erdman, J. I. 1983. Assessing the purposes of early field experiences. *Journal of Teacher Education* 34 (4): 27–31.

Erdman, J. K. 1990. Curriculum and community: A feminist perspective. In *Teaching and thinking about curriculum: Critical inquiries,* edited by J. T. Sears and J. D. Marshall. New York: Teachers College Press.

Feiman-Nemser, S., and M. Buchmann. 1985. Pitfalls of experience in teacher preparation. *Teachers College Record* 87 (1): 53–65.

Forman, E. A., and C. B. Cazden. 1985. Exploring Vygotskian perspectives in education: The cognitive value of peer interaction. In *Culture, communication, and cognition: Vygotskian perspectives,* edited by J. V. Wertsch. New York: Cambridge University Press.

Fromm, E. 1956. *The art of loving.* New York: Harper and Row.

Gallimore, R., S. Dalton, and R. Tharp. 1986. Self-regulation and interactive teaching: The effects of teaching conditions on teachers' cognitive activity. *Elementary School Journal* 86: 613–631.

Garibaldi, A. M. 1992. Preparing teachers for culturally diverse class-rooms. In *Diversity in teacher education: New expectations,* edited by M. E. Dilworth. San Francisco: Jossey-Bass.

Getty Education Institute for the Arts. 1996. *Educating for the workplace through the arts.* Los Angeles: GEIA.

Gibran, K. 1923. *The prophet.* New York: Alfred A. Knopf, Inc.

Glaser, B. G., and A. L. Strauss. 1967. *The discovery of grounded theory: Strategies for qualitative research.* Chicago: Aldine.

Glassman, M. 2001. Dewey and Vygotsky: Society, experience, and inquiry in educational practice. *Educational Researcher* 30 (4): 3–14.

Goldstein, L. S. 1999. The relationship zone: The role of caring relation-ships in the co-construction of mind. *American Educational Research Journal* 36 (3): 647–673.

Goodlad, J. 1990. *Teachers for our nation's schools.* San Francisco: Jossey-Bass.

Goodman, J., and D. R. Fish. 1997. Against-the-grain teacher education: A study of coursework, field experience, and perspectives. *Journal of Teacher Education* 48 (2): 96–107.

Greene, M. 1995. *Releasing the imagination: Essays on education, the arts, and social change.* San Francisco: Jossey-Bass.

Greenfield, P. M. 1984. A theory of the teacher in the learning activities of everyday life. In *Everyday cognition: Its development in social context,* edited by B. Rogoff and J. Lave. Cambridge, Mass.: Harvard University Press.

Grosso de León, A. 2001. *Higher education's challenge: New teacher education models for a new century.* New York: Carnegie Corpora-tion of New York.

Grumet, M. R. 1981. Restitution and reconstruction of educational experience: An autobiographical method for curriculum theory. In *Rethinking curriculum studies: A radical approach,* edited by M. Lawn and L. Barton. New York: Wiley.

———. 1988. *Bitter milk: Women and teaching.* Amherst, Mass.: University of Massachusetts Press.

Hale, J. 1991. The transmission of cultural values to young African American children. *Young Children* 46 (6): 7–15.

Hansen, T., L. Dirckinck-Holmfeld, R. Lewis, and J. Rugelj. 1999. Using telematics for collaborative knowledge construction. In *Collaborative learning: Cognitive and computational approaches,* edited by P. Dillenbourg. Oxford, UK: Elsevier Science.

Hartup, W. W. 1985. Relationships and their significance in cognitive development. In *Social relationships and cognitive development,* edited by R. A. Hinde, A. Perret-Clermont, and J. Stevenson-Hinde. Oxford, UK: Clarendon Press.

Hausfather, S. J. 1996. Vygotsky and schooling: Creating a social context for learning. *Action in Teacher Education* 18 (2): 1–10.

Henson, A., V. Koivu-Rybicki, D. Madigan, and J. A. Muchmore. 2000. Researching teaching through collaborative inquiry with outside researchers. In *Researching teaching: Exploring teacher development through reflexive inquiry,* edited by A. L. Cole and J. G. Knowles. Boston: Allyn and Bacon.

Hodapp, R. M., E. C. Goldfield, and C. J. Boyatzis. 1984. The use of effectiveness of maternal scaffolding in mother-infant games. *Child Development* 55 (3): 772–781.

Hulsebosch, P., and M. Koerner. 1994. A feminist view of foundations of education. *Teaching Education* 6 (2): 51–58.

Jackson, P. W. 1968. *Life in classrooms.* New York: Holt, Rinehart, and Winston.

Jacob, E. 1992. Culture, context, and cognition. In *The handbook of qualitative research in education,* edited by M. D. LeCompte, W. L. Millroy, and J. Preissle. San Diego, Calif.: Academic Press.

Jarchow, E., R. Midkiff, and S. Pickert. 1998. *Practical lessons to promote a global perspective in elementary education.* Washington, D.C.: American Association of Colleges for Teacher Education.

John-Steiner, V. 1985. *Notebooks of the mind: Explorations of thinking.* New York: Harper and Row Publishers.

————. 1989. Beyond the transmission of knowledge: A Vygotskian perspective on creativity. In *The university of the future,* edited by R. Bjornson and M. R. Waldman. Columbus, Ohio: Center for Comparative Studies in the Humanities, Ohio State University.

————.2000. *Creative collaboration.* New York: Oxford University Press.

Keirsey, D., and M. Bates. 1984. *Please understand me: Character and temperament types.* Del Mar, Calif.: Prometheus Nemesis Book Company.

Kincheloe, J. K. 1991. *Teachers as researchers: Qualitative inquiry as a path to empowerment.* London, UK: Falmer Press.

Knowles, J. G., and A. L. Cole. 1998. Setting and defining the context of reform. In *The heart of the matter: Teacher educators and teacher education reform,* edited by A. L. Cole, R. Elijah, and J. G. Knowles. San Francisco: Caddo Gap Press.

Knowles, J. G., and A. L. Cole (with C. S. Presswood). 1994. *Through preservice teachers' eyes: Exploring field experiences through narrative and inquiry.* New York: Macmillan College Publishing Company.

Kozulin, A. 1999. *Vygotsky's psychology: A biography of ideas.* Cambridge, Mass.: Harvard University Press.

Langer, S. 1953. *Feeling and form.* New York: Scribner.

Lave, J. 1977. Tailor-made experiments and evaluating the intellectual consequences of apprenticeship training. *Quarterly Newsletter of the Institute for Comparative Human Development* 1: 1–3.

Lave, J., and E. Wenger. 1991. *Situated learning: Legitimate peripheral participation.* New York: Cambridge University Press.

Leont'ev, A. N. 1981. *Problems of the independent mind.* Moscow: Progress Publishers.

Leont'ev, A. N., and A. R. Luria. 1968. The psychological ideas of L. S. Vygotskii. In *The historical roots of contemporary psychology,* edited by B. B. Wolman. New York: Harper and Row.

Levin, R. A. 1990. Recurring themes and variations. In *Places where teachers are taught,* edited by J. I. Goodlad, R. Soder, and K. A. Sirotnik. San Francisco: Jossey-Bass.

Lortie, D. C. 1975. *Schoolteacher: A sociological study.* Chicago: University of Chicago Press.

Macedo, D. 1994. Preface. In *Conscientization and resistance,* edited by P. McLaren and C. Lankshear. New York: Routledge.

Manning, B. H., and B. D. Payne. 1993. A Vygotskian-based theory of teacher cognition: Toward the acquisition of mental reflection and self-regulation. *Teaching and Teacher Education* 9 (4): 361–371.

Mayeroff, M. 1971. *On caring.* New York: Harper Perennial.

McNamee, G. D. 1990. Learning to read and write in an inner-city setting: A longitudinal study of community change. In *Vygotsky and education: Instructional implications and applications of sociohistorical psychology,* edited by L. C. Moll. New York: Cambridge University Press.

Miles, M., and A. M. Huberman. 1984. *Qualitative data analysis: A sourcebook of new methods.* Beverly Hills, Calif.: Sage Publications.

Moll, L. C., ed. 1990. *Vygotsky and education: Instructional implications and applications of sociohistorical psychology.* New York: Cambridge University Press.

Moskos, C. C. 1989. *Greek Americans: Struggle and success.* New Brunswick, N.J.: Transaction Publishers.

Neelands, J. 1985. *Making sense of drama.* Portsmouth, N.H.: Heinemann.

Newman, D., P. Griffin, and M. Cole. 1989. *The construction zone: Working for cognitive change in school.* New York: Cambridge University Press.

Newman, F., and L. Holzman. 1993. *Lev Vygotsky: Revolutionary scientist.* New York: Routledge.

Noddings, N. 1992. An ethic of caring and its implications for instructional arrangements. *American Journal of Education* 96 (2): 215–230.

Novak, J. and D. Gowin. 1984. *Learning how to learn.* New York: Cambridge University Press.

Osterman, K. F., and R. B. Kottkamp. 1993. *Reflective practice for educators: Improving schooling through professional development.* Newbury, Calif.: Sage.

Peterson, P. L. 1997. Learning out of school and in: Self and experience at home, school, and work. In *Learning from our lives: Women, research, and autobiography in education,* edited by A. Neumann and P. L. Peterson. New York: Teachers College Press.

Pinar, W. F., and M. R. Grumet. 1976. *Toward a poor curriculum.* Dubuque, Iowa: Kendall/Hunt Publishing.

Popkewitz, T. S. 1999. Dewey, Vygotsky, and the social administration of the individual: Constructivist pedagogy as systems of ideas in historical spaces. *American Educational Research Journal* 35 (4): 535–570.

Portes, P. R. 2001. Cultural and ethnic identity formation from a cultural historical perspective: Expansions on Erikson and Vygotsky's contributions. Paper presented at the Annual Meeting of the American Educational Research Association, Seattle, Wash.

Posner, G. J. 1996. *Field experience: A guide to reflective teaching.* White Plains, N.Y.: Longman.

Pugach, M. C., and L. J. Johnson. 1990. Developing reflective practice through structured dialogue. In *Encouraging reflective practice in education: An analysis of issues and programs,* edited by R. T. Clift, W. R. Houston, and M. S. Pugach. New York: Teachers College Press.

Ralph, E. G., C. Kesten, H. Lang, and D. Smith. 1998. Hiring new teachers: What do school districts look for? *Journal of Teacher Education* 49 (1): 47–56.

Ratner, N., and J. Bruner. 1978. Games, social exchange and the acquisition of language. *Journal of Child Language* 5: 391–401.

Resnick, L. B., J. M. Levine, and S. D. Teasley, eds. 1991. *Perspectives on socially shared cognition.* Washington, D.C.: American Psychological Association.

Rios, F. A., J. E. McDaniel, and L. P. Stowell. 1998. Making the path by walking it. In *The heart of the matter: Teacher educators and teacher education reform,* edited by A. L. Cole, R. Elijah, and J. G. Knowles. San Francisco: Caddo Gap Press.

Rogoff, B. 1982. Integrating context and cognitive development. In *Advances in developmental psychology,* edited by M. E. Lamb and A. L. Brown. Vol. 2. Hillsdale, N.J.: Lawrence Erlbaum.

———. 1986. Adult assistance of children's learning. In *The contexts of school based literacy,* edited by T. E. Raphael. New York: Random House.

———.1987. The joint socialization of development by young children and adults. In *Social influences and behavior,* edited by M. Lewis and S. Feinman. New York: Plenum.

Rogoff, B., and W. Gardner. 1984. Adult guidance of cognitive development. In *Everyday cognition: Its development in social context,* edited by B. Rogoff, and J. Lave. Cambridge, Mass.: Harvard University Press.

Rogoff, B., C. Malkin, and K. Gilbride. 1984. Interaction with babies as guidance in development. In *Children's learning in the "zone of proximal development,* edited by B. Rogoff and J. Wertsch. San Francisco: Jossey-Bass.

Rouvelas, M. 1993. *A guide to Greek traditions and customs in America.* Bethesda, Md.: Nea Attiki Press.

Samaras, A. P. 1984. *Teaching children from a Greek culture: A multicultural workshop for educators.* Annapolis, Md.: Board of Education of Anne Arundel County Schools.

———. 1989. Creativity is spelled with 3 R's: Respect, responsivity, and reciprocity. Paper presented at the annual conference of the Maryland Association for the Education of Young Children, Towson, Md.

———. 1990a. Beyond "scaffolding": The role of mediation in preschoolers' self-regulation of model-consultation with microcomputer puzzles. Paper presented at the annual meeting of the American Educational Research Association, Boston, Mass. ERIC Document Reproduction Service No. ED 321 888.

———. 1990b. Transitions to competence: The role of mediation in preschoolers' self-regulation with a microcomputer-based problem-solving task. Ph.D. diss., University of Maryland, College Park.

———. 1991. Transitions to competence: An investigation of adult mediation in preschoolers' self-regulation with a microcomputer-based problem-solving task. *Early Education and Development* 2 (3): 181–196.

———. 1994a. *Into the mainstream: Remembering ethnic life in Annapolis, 1945–1965. A panel discussion with reflections from members of the Italian, Jewish, African-American and Greek communities.* Annapolis, Md.: Maryland Humanities Council, National Endowment for the Humanities and Congregation Kneseth Israel.

———. 1994b. Show and tell those theories! *Day Care and Early Education* 2 (1): 21–23.

———. 1995. My journey to Ithaca: Reflections of a teacher educator. *Teaching Education* 7 (1): 96–101.

———. 1996. Children's computers. *Childhood Education* 72 (3): 133–136.

———. 1997. Using the Vygotskian approach in the teacher education classroom. Paper presented at the Lilly Conference on Excellence in College and University Teaching, Towson, Md.

———. 1998a. Birthing legitimate research: The morality of self-study in teacher education. Paper presented at the annual meeting of the American Association for Colleges of Teacher Education, New Orleans, La.

————. 1998b. Finding my way: Teaching methods courses from a sociocultural perspective. In *The heart of the matter: Teacher educators and teacher education reform,* edited by A. L. Cole, R. Elijah, and J. G. Knowles. San Francisco: Caddo Gap Press.

————, 2000a. Scaffolding preservice teachers' learning. In *Innovations in practice: Promoting meaningful learning for early childhood professionals,* edited by N. J. Yelland. Washington, D.C.: The National Association for the Education of Young Children.

————. 2000b. When is a practicum productive?: A study in learning to plan. *Action in Teacher Education* 22 (2): 100–115.

Samaras, A. P., S. L. Francis, Y. D. Holt, T. W. Jones, D. S. Martin, J. L. Thompson, and A. R. Tom. 1999. Lived experiences and reflections of joint state-NCATE reviews. *The Teacher Educator* 35 (1): 68–83.

Samaras, A. P., and S. Gismondi. 1998. Scaffolds in the field: Vygotskian interpretation in a teacher education program. *Teaching and Teacher Education* 14 (7): 715–733.

Samaras, A. P., B. J. Howard, and C. Wende. 2000. Kyoto Redoux: Assessment of an environmental science collaborative learning project for undergraduate, non-science majors. *Canadian Journal of Environmental Education* 5: 26–47.

Samaras, A. P., and S. Pheiffer. 1996. I can see it now! Using the visual arts to teach about diversity in social studies. Paper presented at the annual conference of the National Council for the Social Studies, Washington, D.C.

Samaras, A. P., and B. Pour. 1992. Playing literacy: Integrating children's literature, drama, and movement. Paper presented at the Association for Childhood Education International, Washington Metro Branch Conference, Arlington, Va.

————. 1993. Extending literacy through the arts. Paper presented at the annual conference of the National Council for Teachers of English, Spring, Richmond, Va.

Samaras, A. P., with R. L. Reed. 2000. Transcending traditional boundaries through drama: Interdisciplinary teaching and perspective-taking. Paper presented at the bi-annual conference of the Self-Study in Teacher Education Practices, East Sussex, England.

————. 2001a. Renaissance faculty: Drama and education departments integrate the arts in teacher preparation. Paper presented at the annual meeting of the American Association of Colleges for Teacher Education, Dallas, Tex.

————. 2001b. Will you please cooperate? Drama and education departments integrate the arts in teacher preparation. Paper presented at the annual meeting of the American Educational Research Association, Seattle, Wash.

Samaras, A. P., S. A. Straits, and S. S. Patrick. 1998. Collaborating through movement across disciplines and schools. *Teaching Education* 9 (2): 11–20.

Samaras, A. P., N. E. Taylor, and B. Kelly. 1994. Teachers teaching teachers. *Momentum* 25 (3): 67–71.

Samaras, A. P., and J. C. Wilson. 1999. Am I invited?: Perspectives of family involvement with technology in inner city schools. *Urban Education* 34 (4): 499–530.

Sarason, S. B. 1999. *Teaching as a performing art.* New York: Teachers College Press.

Schwab, J. J. 1973. The practical 3: Translation into curriculum. *School Review* 81 (4): 501–522.

Short, L. G., and C. L. Burke. 1989. New potentials for teacher education: Teaching and learning as inquiry. *Elementary School Journal* 90 (2): 191–206.

Shulman, L. S. 1986. Those who understand: Knowledge growth in teaching. *Educational Researcher* 15 (2): 4–21.

————. 1987. Knowledge in teaching: Foundations of the new reform. *Harvard Educational Review* 57 (1): 1–22.

Smith, B. O. 1980. Pedagogical education: How about reform? *Phi Delta Kappan* 62 (2): 87–91.

Spolin, V. 1999. *Improvisation for the theater.* Evanston, Ill.: Northwestern University Press.

Stanislavsky, K. 1989. *An actor prepares.* New York: Routledge.

Sternberg, P. 1998. *Theatre for conflict resolution: In the classroom and beyond.* Portsmouth, N.H.: Heinemann.

Stone, C. A. 1985. Vygotsky's developmental model and the concept of proleptic instruction: Some implications for theory and research in the field of learning disabilities. *Research Communications in Psychology, Psychiatry and Behavior* 10 (1 and 2): 129–152.

Sumara, D. J. and T. R. Carson. 1997. Reconceptualizing action research as a living practice. *Action research as a living practice.* edited by T. R. Carson and D. J. Sumara. New York: Peter Lang Publishers.

Taylor, P. 1996. Doing reflective practitioner research in arts education. In *Researching drama and arts education: Paradigms and possibilities,* edited by P. Taylor. London: Falmer Press.

————. 1998. Redcoats and patriots: Reflective practice in drama and social studies. Portsmouth, N.H.: Heinemann.

Taylor, N. E., A. P. Samaras, and A. Gay. 1994. Making connections: Aligning theory and field practice. Paper presented at the annual meeting of the American Association of Colleges for Teacher Education, Chicago, Ill. ERIC Document Reproduction Service No. ED 367 597.

Taylor, N. E., and J. C. Wilson. 1997. Teaching in culturally diverse contexts: Findings from a reflective teacher education program. Paper presented at the annual meeting of the American Association of Colleges for Teacher Education, Chicago, Ill. ERIC Document Reproduction Service No. ED 413 327.

Tharp, R. G., and R. Gallimore. 1990. *Rousing minds to life: Teaching, learning, and schooling in social context.* New York: Cambridge University Press.

Thomas, D. 1985. About teaching and teachers: The torpedo's touch. *Harvard Educational Review* 55 (2): 220–222.

Treiber, F. 1984. Ineffective teaching: Can we learn from it? *Journal of Teacher Education* 35 (5): 45–47.

Tudge, J., and B. Rogoff. 1989. Peer influences on cognitive development: Piagetian and Vygotskian perspectives. In *Interaction in human development,* edited by M. M. Bornstein and J. S. Bruner. Hillsdale, N.J.: Lawrence Erlbaum.

U. S. Department of Education. 1994. *Goals 2000: National education goals.* Washington, D.C.: U. S. Government Printing Office.

————. 1999. President Clinton sends FY2000 education budget to Congress. *Community Update* 65. Washington, D.C.: U.S. Government Printing Office.

Valli, L. 1990. Moral approaches to reflective practice. In *Encouraging reflective practice in education,* edited by R. T. Clift, W. R. Houston, and M. C. Pugach. New York: Teachers College Press.

Valsiner, J., and R. van der Veer. 2000. *The social mind: Construction of the idea.* New York: Cambridge University Press.

van der Veer, R., and J. Valsiner. 1991. *Understanding Vygotsky: A quest for synthesis.* Cambridge, Mass.: Blackwell.

van Manen, M. 1977. Linking ways of knowing with ways of being practical. *Curriculum Inquiry* 6 (3): 205–228.

Verducci, S. 1998. A moral method? A look at how the practice of method acting can inform efforts to cultivate empathy in students. Paper presented at the annual meeting of the American Educational Research Association, San Diego, Calif.

Vygotsky, L. S. [1934] 1962. *Thought and language.* Edited and trans lated by E. Hanfmann and G. Vokar. Cambridge, Mass.: Massachusetts Institute of Technology Press.

———. [1960] 1981. The genesis of higher mental functions. In *The concept of activity in Soviet psychology,* edited by J. V. Wertsch. Armonk, N.Y.: M. E. Sharpe.

———. 1978. *Mind in society: The development of higher psychological processes.* Edited by M. Cole, V. John-Steiner, S. Scribner, and E. Souberman. Cambridge, Mass.: Harvard University Press.

———. [1926] 1997. *Educational psychology.* Introduction by V. V. Davydov and R. Silverman. Boca Raton, Fla: St. Lucie Press.

Wagner, B. J. 1998. *Educational drama and language arts: What research shows.* Portsmouth, N.H.: Heinemann.

Wasser, J. D., and L. Bresler. 1996. Working in the interpretive zone: Conceptualizing collaboration in qualitative research teams. *Educational Researcher* 25 (5): 5–15.

Weiler, K. 1988. *Women teaching for change: Gender, class and power.* South Hadley, Mass.: Bergin and Garvey Publishers.

Wells, G. 2000. Dialogic inquiry in education: Building on the legacy of Vygotsky. In *Vygotskian perspectives on literacy research: Constructing meaning through collaborative inquiry,* edited by C. D. Lee and P. Smagorinsky. Cambridge, UK: Cambridge University Press.

Wertsch, J. V. 1984. The zone of proximal development: Some conceptual issues. In *Children's learning in the "zone of proximal development,"* edited by B. Rogoff and J. V. Wertsch. San Francisco: Jossey-Bass.

———. 1985. *Vygotsky and the social formation of mind.* Cambridge, Mass.: Harvard University Press.

———. 1991. *Voices of the mind: A sociocultural approach to mediated action.* Cambridge, Mass.: Harvard University Press.

Wertsch, J. V., and M. Hickman. 1987. Problem solving in social interaction: A microgenetic analysis. In *Social and functional approaches to language and thought,* edited by M. Hickman. Orlando, Fla: Academic Press.

Wertsch, J. V., and J. Younnis. 1987. Contextualizing the investigator: The case of developmental psychology. *Human Development* 30: 18–31.

Westerman, D. A. 1991. Expert and novice teacher decision making. *Journal of Teacher Education* 42 (4): 292–305.

Wineburg, S. 1997. Collaboration, and the quandaries of assessment in a rapidly changing world. *Phi Delta Kappan* 79 (1): 59–65.

Wood, D., J. S. Bruner, and G. Ross. 1976. The role of tutoring in problem solving. *Journal Child Psychology and Psychiatry* 17: 89–100.

Wood, D., and H. Wood. 1996. Vygotsky, tutoring and learning. *Oxford Review of Education* 22 (1): 5–16.

Wright, J., and A. Samaras. 1986. Play worlds and microworlds. In *Young children and microcomputers,* edited by P. F. Campbell and G. G. Fein. Englewood Cliffs, New Jersey: Prentice Hall.

Wright, S. 1997. Learning how to learn: The arts as core in an emergent curriculum. *Childhood Education* 73 (6): 361–365.

Zeichner, K. 1995. Beyond the great divide of teacher research and academic research. *Teachers and Teaching: Theory and Practice* 1 (2): 153–172.

———. 1999. The new scholarship in teacher education. *Educational Researcher* 28 (9): 4–15.

Zeichner, K. M., and D. P. Liston. 1996. *Reflective teaching: An introduction.* Mahwah, N.J.: Lawrence Erlbaum.

Studies in the Postmodern Theory of Education

General Editors
Joe L. Kincheloe & Shirley R. Steinberg

Counterpoints publishes the most compelling and imaginative books being written in education today. Grounded on the theoretical advances in criticalism, feminism, and postmodernism in the last two decades of the twentieth century, Counterpoints engages the meaning of these innovations in various forms of educational expression. Committed to the proposition that theoretical literature should be accessible to a variety of audiences, the series insists that its authors avoid esoteric and jargonistic languages that transform educational scholarship into an elite discourse for the initiated. Scholarly work matters only to the degree it affects consciousness and practice at multiple sites. Counterpoints' editorial policy is based on these principles and the ability of scholars to break new ground, to open new conversations, to go where educators have never gone before.

For additional information about this series or for the submission of manuscripts, please contact:

> Joe L. Kincheloe & Shirley R. Steinberg
> c/o Peter Lang Publishing, Inc.
> 275 Seventh Avenue, 28th floor
> New York, New York 10001

To order other books in this series, please contact our Customer Service Department:

> (800) 770-LANG (within the U.S.)
> (212) 647-7706 (outside the U.S.)
> (212) 647-7707 FAX

Or browse online by series:

> www.peterlangusa.com

DATE DUE
